Praise for
THE GREAT PEACE

USA Today, "5 Books Not to Miss"
Good Morning America, "33 Books to Heat Up Your July"
NY POST, "30 Best Books on Our Summer Reading List in 2021"
KatieCouric.com, Zibby Owens' "8 Emotional Books That Made Me
Really Feel"

"Powerful... [as] an abuse survivor, Mena bares her soul on the page to show others that there's always a light at the end of the tunnel—even her own."

—*Good Morning America*

"I walked away from her book thinking it was a very, very timely memoir in this larger discussion of female strength and finding your voice...She's overcome so much and come out on the other end in the best possible place."

—Thora Birch, in the *Los Angeles Times*

"Suvari is unflinching in detailing the sex, drugs, abuse and toxic relationships that afflicted her adolescence and young adulthood even as she was becoming a star, [but] *The Great Peace* is not a sordid tell-all or Hollywood expose. Instead, Suvari has written something more personal, a sort of diary of her spiritual journey...Though ultimately hopeful, *The Great Peace* is often a harrowing read."

—*USA Today*

"Mena Suvari has decided to tell everything...[this book] spares no details."

—*Vanity Fair*

"Suvari pulls absolutely no punches in this raw exploration of a Hollywood childhood full of sexual abuse, emotional abandonment and drug addiction—and reveals how she built a new life on her own terms."

—*NY POST*

"The details are harrowing, but the overall effect of her writing is strangely intoxicating...In unfussy prose...Suvari transports the reader...What's most impressive is Suvari's willingness to admit to mistakes and even at times risk coming off as unlikable. She wants people to read and relate to her story, but beyond the notion that the truth has set her free, there isn't a didactic moral takeaway."

—*Jezebel*

"[A] soul-baring memoir..."

—*Los Angeles Daily News*

"A powerful read that—much like Sharon Stone's *The Beauty of Living Twice*—will make you see its author in a different, perhaps more forgiving light."

—*Total Film*

"Suvari's bracing tale of abusive patterns and building new beginnings is wrenching, potent, and ultimately inspirational."

—*Kirkus*, starred review

"Fearless and forthright...Using the wisdom that she's gathered from excruciating breakups, near-death experiences, the loss of a parent, and more, Suvari proves to be an exceptionally strong narrator whose memoir will offer solace and companionship to readers who might feel isolated and alone...An honest and unadorned Hollywood confessional that casts a light on the darkness behind the scenes."

—*Library Journal*

"Haunting...While the experiences she details are devastating, her ability to weave them into a narrative of empowerment is what makes this so moving. In bringing her struggles to light, Suvari reclaims her story and will surely inspire others to do the same."

—*Publishers Weekly*

"A harrowing, often painful story of the all-too-prevalent ways young women are preyed upon, and the work it takes to find hope and healing."

—*Booklist*

THE
GREAT
PEACE

THE
GREAT
PEACE

A Memoir

MENA SUVARI

hachette
BOOKS

New York

Hachette Books
Hachette Book Group
1290 Avenue of the Americas
New York, NY 10104
HachetteBooks.com
Twitter.com/HachetteBooks
Instagram.com/HachetteBooks

First Trade Paperback Edition: July 2022

Published by Hachette Books, an imprint of Perseus Books, LLC, a subsidiary of Hachette Book Group, Inc. The Hachette Books name and logo is a trademark of the Hachette Book Group.

The Hachette Speakers Bureau provides a wide range of authors for speaking events. To find out more, go to www.hachettespeakersbureau.com or call (866) 376-6591.

The publisher is not responsible for websites (or their content) that are not owned by the publisher.

Print book interior design by Amy Quinn.

Library of Congress Control Number: 2021935699

ISBNs: 978-0-306-87452-9 (hardcover), 978-0-306-87450-5 (trade paperback), 978-0-306-87449-9 (ebook), 978-0-306-82618-4 (B&N signed edition), 978-0-306-82617-7 (signed edition)

Printed in the United States of America

LSC-C

Printing 1, 2022

Dedicated to the Power above.

CONTENTS

AUTHOR'S NOTE

I NEVER INTENDED TO WRITE THIS BOOK; IT WASN'T EVEN SOMETHING I HAD PREVIously thought about, being an author.

I spent almost my entire life feeling disgusted, ashamed, and in denial about what happened to me and what I had allowed myself to do and be a part of. Then one day, I stopped. I stopped running away and I looked at myself. I looked into the pain and what I saw was that I was ready to leave it all behind and heal.

It hasn't been easy to revisit all of this. It has brought up emotions that I thought I had firmly dealt with only to find out that I had actually expended great energy avoiding them. I see now how the experience of writing this book and forcing myself to finally deal with the truth has also been the greatest gift. Going back allowed me to heal and regain my power. Hopefully it will inspire others to do the same. Many of us believe that we are alone in our hurt and should suffer in isolation. In truth, we are all connected, and the greatest gift we can give to one another is sharing our experiences and collected wisdom.

There is strength in numbers. My hope is that this book can provide companionship to those who feel alone and lonely and don't think anyone else is there for them, as I felt for so much of my life. I want it to serve as the flickering light at the end of a dark road showing there is a way out. And there is.

Mena Suvari

THE
GREAT
PEACE

INTRODUCTION

The Great Peace was the title of a book of poetry and stories I wrote in my late teens. It included some drawings, too. The irony of the title is that the material in it painted a portrait of a young woman dealing with large sweeps of inner turmoil, anything but a great peace was, I suppose, what I sought. I carried the book with me as if it were a lifeline until I moved one too many times and it ended up at the bottom of a box in a storage unit, where it remained conveniently out of sight and ignored but never altogether forgotten.

The storage unit was near where I grew up, which was strangely fitting, because where better to bury all those painful experiences than where they happened?

That book and those writings, they were such a desperate plea to the world, to the universe, to anyone who might throw me a lifeline.

I never expected I would be the one to respond. But while visiting my husband in Canada in 2018, I decided I wanted to redecorate our home. On the days when Mike went to work, I sat with my morning coffee and looked at pictures of beautiful rooms. I wanted an organic and natural look, something that felt grounding, earthy, and real. More wood, less leather and chrome.

Once I got back to LA, I went to the storage unit to inventory the furniture and sift through the boxes. I decided to sell everything and use the money to finance my new dream interior. The unit was jammed with stuff. Years earlier, following the end of a relationship, I left the house where I had lived and put everything into there. It was typical of me. Just bid adieu to a bad situation, or two or three. My version of therapy was a garage, a padlock, and driving like a bat out of hell in the opposite direction.

"God, I can't even remember all that's in there," I told Mike on the phone, though that wasn't true. I knew where the storage unit was located and what was inside. This was confirmed as soon as the metal door creaked open and light poured into the dark space. Furniture. Boxes. My life was staring at me, waiting to greet me again. *Hello, Mena. We've been waiting for you.* I moved things around, marveling at how much shit I had amassed. I felt good about selling this stuff. It was the smart move.

Pushing things around opened up a path toward the back and I came upon a plastic bin. I remembered this one. Inside was my diary, my poetry binder titled *The Great Peace*, and my art book filled with drawings and collages. I had poured my heart into these books until I . . . I couldn't remember why I had stopped. Or where in my life I had stopped.

Later, I brought the bin back to my home office. And as I pulled out the books, I thought about how strange it was that many of my old memories remained as vivid as my most recent television binge but then suddenly had huge blank spots, the screen just going black. I took a seat and opened my diary. So many of the entries instantly took me back to the moment they were written. I wrote about people letting me down and wanting to escape into nature. I wiped a tear from my eye. Then, after dozens of entries, the pages went blank. It was full stop.

Until I found a letter that was glued onto the inside of the back cover. I unfolded the pale yellow construction paper card and saw a note written in a beautiful cursive, signed at the end with an Estonian quote, and adorned with an angel sticker, as if to welcome the reader who found it. How ironic and amazing that *that* reader happened to be me. I read two lines before I stopped and gasped. I was reading my suicide note.

That day came rushing back to me. I wrote the letter after things had gotten bad. My family had come to an end and I couldn't take any more abuse from the outside. Frail, weak, and lost, I was tired of holding on. I had no idea how I made it through that despair only to enter the gates of a new hell, but as I thought back to what was happening then and why I hadn't taken my life, I remembered the way I would find the tiniest glimmer of hope that my life could get even slightly better, and believe it. I clung to that belief with all my might.

That's how it was. Deep down, in the marrow of my bones, where no one could get no matter how they ripped into my flesh, I held on to my dreams and the hope I had for myself. I looked for the beauty that was around me, compelled to see it, no matter how hard it was to find. I knew there was a glimmer of light that I could follow through the darkness. I never got the apologies I wanted from the people who hurt me, but I came to understand they were unnecessary for my well-being. I needed only one person's forgiveness.

This is her story.

I.

The thoughts of the silent in heart,
Turning while wandering, then tearing apart.
Apart from the norm that used to be,
  • Something that is routine to you and me.

II.

Call to the skies that lie in the heavens above.
Raise your arms and offer your love.
Acceptance will then come to thee.
  • Something that is routine to you and me.

III.

Gaze upon the mirror of sea,
Submerge your thoughts for eternity.
The moonlight subjects to set one free,
  • Something that is routine to you and me.

IV.

The gentle sways that move your soul,
Around and spinning 'till death takes its toll.
The shadow that appears, not hard to see,
  • Is something that is routine to you and me.

11/14/95

MENA'S CORNER

Even before I arrived in this world, my ability has never been in doubt. One morning when my mother was newly pregnant with me but didn't know it yet, she descended the stairs in our home in her stocking feet with the youngest of my three older brothers, a baby at the time, in her arms, she slipped and fell.

Rather than grab the rail to break her fall as she might have if solo, she clutched my brother tightly to her chest and submitted to the loss of balance and pull of gravity, rolling down the last few steps, before coming to a hard landing at the bottom. My brother was unscathed, but my mother was badly bruised and required a trip to the emergency room for good measure. According to X-rays, she had miraculously avoided breaking any bones.

Apparently she wasn't out of the woods. At a party, weeks later, she started to hemorrhage and subsequently learned she was pregnant. She immediately questioned the doctor about the effect of the X-rays. She worried they had damaged the fetus, caused her to bleed, and endangered the viability of her pregnancy. She was sure she was losing the baby if she hadn't already lost it.

The doctor reassured her everything was okay, and it was. I held on, and when I was born, on February 13, 1979, her doctor declared, "Well, she's a little small, but she's got everything. You got your girl."

We lived in a beautiful, regal home built in 1870 off Ruggles Avenue in Newport, Rhode Island. My parents moved into this grand residence shortly after the birth of my second-oldest brother. It included a ballroom and its own name, Hilltop. My father, a psychiatrist, was in his early sixties when I joined the family, and my mother, almost thirty years his junior, was a homemaker. I grew up thinking all of life was magical.

We lived on four acres of land. My brothers built a tree fort on one end of the property where we were surrounded by woods. We walked around all day picking blackberries, which we cleaned and smothered with cream later on and ate for dessert. I wanted to be an archeologist and I established a four-foot dig in a corner of the backyard, which I tended to every morning after breakfast. I collected all my treasures, mainly china, but also a real bullet. I glued these precious fragments together in an effort to re-create the lives and lifestyle of the families who had lived there before me.

I was most content when I was on my own and able to teach myself. My mother discovered that I could read one day when we were sitting in a dentist's office waiting room and I picked up a book and started to read it. I was photographed on the first day of first grade at the New School holding a copy of *Island of the Blue Dolphins*. There were moments when teachers weren't sure "what to do with me," as they said, because I finished my work so quickly. Since they didn't want me "disrupting the rest of the class"—again, their words—I was sent to second grade for reading and other subjects.

My mother came to school one day and found they had sent me to the library to sit in an area they deemed "Mena's Corner." This was where I read and entertained myself while the rest of class went on. My mother was infuriated. People didn't know what to do with me, so they set me aside in whatever way was most convenient.

Later, my mother said I'd been invited to join Mensa, but she held me back out of fear that being too smart would make me seem too different. Decisions like this backfired and ultimately made me feel separate from the crowd and never part of the norm, no matter how hard my mother encouraged me to "fit in."

To that end, she got me into modeling. I became a client of a modeling agency in Boston and they created a "go-see" card for me. It included a cute little head shot. I worked right away on a regional commercial for a politician in Rhode Island, but once I lost my two front teeth, the agency put me on a hiatus.

Not a problem.

RICH BITCH

When I was eight years old, my parents wanted to move to a warmer climate and they chose St. John in the Virgin Islands. I went there with one of my brothers and my mother, who opened a tiny general store in town and supervised construction of our new home right on the bay. My father and my other two brothers stayed back to watch over Hilltop. My parents hired a tutor to teach me and my brother so we could keep up our studies, but she went rogue and my brother and I found ourselves not attending school for the year.

Somehow I convinced my mother to let me help her run her store, which she'd named Mena. I maintained it would provide enough education until we could find another option. I used my childhood cuteness to great effect on the tourists who wandered in during their strolls from their cruise ships. If not in the store, I explored the bay where we lived, collecting shells, swimming in the tide pools, and learning about all kinds of magnificent creatures I'd never seen. I stepped on so many sea urchins in the process of collecting shells that my father, at one point, said he wasn't going to take them out of my feet for me anymore.

One of my favorite things to do with my brother was to walk along the reef to the hotel at the center of the bay and sneak in to use their pool. Around the pool area, they would serve little hors d'oeuvres and my brother and I spent hours hanging out there, pretending we were hotel guests and enjoying all of the luxuries. Acting came naturally, I guess. One day I was swimming in the pool when I saw a ginormous bow attached to the head of a beautiful woman. It was bright purple and I had never seen such glamour. Full of excitement and confidence, I swam over to her and as I got closer I said, "I know who you are!"

She asked, "What's your name?" I told her, and then she smiled. "Well, now I know who *you* are."

She was Whitney Houston, and she was as lovely as everyone ever said. It was an incredible moment, made more so by the struggles I later imagined she ultimately succumbed to, which were more real to me than I would have preferred.

Our house in St. John was perpetually under construction, progress being imperceptible for long stretches that first year. It turned out there was a reason. Our contractor was using the money my father sent him on drugs and partying. The attempt at island life a failure, we returned to Rhode Island and lived at Hilltop for a while longer. Then money issues caught up with us. The funds squandered in St. John combined with my father's dwindling practice (he saw a few patients in our ballroom) and an unsuccessful attempt to sell Hilltop would eventually force us to move into a smaller residence in another part of town.

Like most kids, I possessed the resiliency and optimism of youth, something perhaps better called blissful ignorance. While in St. John, I had weathered news of the death back home of our beloved family dog, Jesse, who was poisoned by a neighbor, something I still hear about and that makes me wonder what kind of cruelty drives a human to such a dastardly action. Back at Hilltop, my brothers and I played in our yard and rode our bikes to the park, where we amused ourselves on the swings and slide. I befriended a girl who became jealous of another friend I made, and her older brother made a point of threatening and bullying me every time he saw me in the neighborhood.

One day, as I was riding back home from the market, they came upon me on a side street and cornered me. Her brother picked up the front wheel of my bike, which threw me off the back and onto the ground. As I got up, he slapped me across my face calling me a "rich bitch," and proceeded to tell me that I wasn't allowed to ride my bike in the neighborhood anymore and if he saw me out, he would hurt me even more.

From then on, I was terrified to go out. I took long back routes to the market or anywhere else I had to go in order to avoid him.

It wasn't enough. I was pedaling back from the market one afternoon and as I came back up to my street, I looked to my left toward the park and there they were: the brother with his friend on their respective ten-speeds. I knew I was done for. As they raced toward me, I pedaled as fast as I could and thought I might be able to make it home. But then the chain came off my bike. I couldn't believe it.

I tried to coast. I was so damn scared of what they were going to do to me. They'd hit me before and promised worse the next time. I moved my body back and forth, trying to urge more momentum into the bike. Somehow I made it to our gravel driveway, swerving in just as they were about to catch me. Out of nowhere my brother appeared, the one just above me in age, and the other kids saw him, too. They turned around and rode away.

I was an emotional wreck. I told my brother all about the situation and not long after that day he did one of the most amazing brotherly things of my life. He got on his bike and rode with me to the neighborhood where the sister and brother lived, and we parked ourselves in front of those two creeps' house and waited for them to see us. Without uttering a word, my brother let them know the jig was up. I remember the look on the bully brother's face: astonishment, helplessness, and surrender. It was, indeed, over, but it was followed by a stern reminder I'd always heard from my father: "You ask for trouble, you get it."

Soon after that confrontation, we moved to an apartment near the marina and then to a small home in another suburban neighborhood, where my brother and I cut down our own little Christmas trees for our bedrooms. At Hilltop we'd usually had a gigantic one for the whole family, but I think all the relocations and a slight awareness of my parents' struggle to hang on to some kind of stability left me always trying to create a little world of my own that was safe and comfortable and filled with the wonder of my early childhood there.

Whether or not I was aware of it, forces much greater than me took me away from that place I was desperately trying to re-create, and more so as time went on, until it was a dot on the horizon that seemed like a dream rather than anything that had once been real. Good or bad, life was an inevitable sailing away from childhood. I just wish it had happened to me more gradually instead of through such forceful jolts.

NO ONE TOLD ME

After I finished fifth grade, we moved to Charleston, South Carolina, where I started middle school at Ashley Hall, an all-girls school steeped in Southern traditions. We had visited my brother at military school in Virginia Beach, and my parents had grown fond of the South during frequent trips to see my ailing grandmother. Before she passed away, they started looking for a place of our own. At first, we lived in a back guesthouse of a beautifully remodeled traditional Charleston house in the center of town.

But Charleston was a place rooted in tradition and history. And because I wasn't from there and came from the North, I was instantly branded "the Yankee," and it was easily decided that I wouldn't fit in, no matter how hard I tried. I poured all of my energy into my studies because that was the one thing I could control and lose myself in. I spent a lot of time with myself, riding my bike around to see the few friends I did make, including a new girl who came midyear and said, "I'm glad we're friends, because when I first came here, everyone told me not to be friends with you."

I felt pretty lost and such pressure to fit into a box I couldn't squeeze into. I wanted to be expressive and weird, but I felt I needed to shop at the Gap and Express in order to be accepted. My mother even decorated my room in all Laura Ashley, and I hated it. I felt stifled. I was never the frilly, delicate girl everyone expected and wanted me to be. But I learned to pretend and play the game. I made one good friend while I was there, a girl named

14

Jennie. One day I invited her to sit next to me in class and we became fast friends who remain close to this day.

I have no explanation why that was, but I was grateful. Jennie was fun and sweet and smart. She knew everyone in Charleston and helped me feel less alone. I feel like she gave me a safe space to be myself and I probably helped her express her wilder, more adventurous side. Her family and their beautiful home downtown reminded me of Hilltop and confirmed my belief that such places were real and possible.

Jennie and I became best friends and soon developed a shared passion for the film *Beaches*. We sang and danced to the songs in the movie, convinced we were just like the two characters with their intensely deep expressions of love and friendship. She was the first of the many friends I would have whose home lives replaced things lacking in my own.

Around this same time I met my middle brother's friend Kenny James Thorn. We were living downtown, in our back guesthouse off Queen Street, and KJ, as he was known, was frequently there, hanging out with my brother. He was my brother's age—about three years older than me—and in high school. I might have been one of the reasons he was at our house. I don't know why he would have been attracted to someone so much younger, but he was, and though it might have annoyed my brother, I didn't mind the attention.

My first hint that he liked me came one night when the three of us were alone at the house. My mother and everyone else had gone out. It was late, and I had said goodnight to the boys and gone to bed. I don't know how long I had been asleep before I was jolted awake to the sound of the Police's song "Roxanne" blasting from my brother's room. It was so loud the speakers might as well have been in my room. Then they burst into my room like naughty pranksters, and the next thing I knew KJ hopped up on my bed and hovered over me.

It was typical adolescent behavior and not that far removed from the way my first so-called boyfriend in grade school let me know he liked me with a sharp kick. He always picked on me, and I hated him for it so much that he became my first kiss.

KJ would be different, very different, in the sense that his "kick" ripped whatever was left of my childhood from me and put it out of reach forever.

I was approaching the end of my twelfth year. We were living downtown while my family built a home in a new subdivision on a lake. It was a busy, consuming time for my parents, who made frequent trips back and forth to check on the work. One morning I woke up in our guesthouse and realized I had started to bleed. It wasn't much at first and I wasn't too alarmed, but I had no idea what was happening since my parents had never spoken to me about the changes I would experience as I began adolescence and my body matured.

However, as the day went on, the flow of blood coming out of me got redder and redder and more and more. Alarmed and afraid, I went into my mother's room. With tears pouring out of my eyes, I told her what was happening and said I thought I was dying. I wish I could say she consoled me and offered comforting, positive reinforcement about becoming a woman and the power and responsibility that went along with that amazing transformation. But she didn't, and I don't know why. Instead, we had a brief, awkward conversation, and I was told to expect more of the same every month.

Needing to look elsewhere for the warmth I craved, I found KJ ready and waiting. He had started writing me love letters that spoke of his deep affection for me. In these letters, he described in great detail what he saw in me and what he loved about me and how much he wanted to be with me. He was clearly obsessed, but it was the kind of attention I wanted as I took this new step into womanhood feeling disappointed in my mother and uncertain and alone.

Here was this guy who thought about my hair, went to sleep thinking about my eyes, woke up hoping to see my smile, and felt like his day was always better if he got even a short glimpse of me. What young, insecure girl wouldn't respond to such positive attention from a boy, and an older one at that? How could I resist?

"I DON'T WANT
TO DO THAT!"

K J called me every day or came over to our house, or both. No one stopped him from being alone with me in my bedroom. No one cautioned me. No one inquired when he became more my friend than my brother's. No one asked what we talked about or what we did together all day. I was always left to my own devices. Even as a small child, I never had a curfew. As I got older, my parents never asked where I was going or who I spent time with. They never peeked in on me and KJ or told me to leave the door open.

Then the new house was completed and we moved in. It was grand and painted canary yellow. My room had its own balcony overlooking the lake and beyond, which was where KJ lived with his parents. They were directly across from us, on the other side of the lake, and had been living there for many years. They had a small white paddleboat. Sometimes KJ took me out on the boat and we pedaled around the lake, where he inevitably steered us out of view and tried to kiss me.

At first I resisted. I wasn't ready the way he was, and I was a little scared, but his persistence and insistence that I was ready (he said he could tell) wore me down until I kissed him back. It began a pattern.

Every day KJ professed his love in some way or another, and I came to trust him as a best friend, protector, and boyfriend, though I was still of the age when I thought of him more as a friend who was a boy than my first steady boyfriend. I was naive and still a kid, almost thirteen but not quite, and caught up and confused by the changes I was experiencing.

I loved to rollerblade. But always geared up with every kind of protective pad imaginable, to the point that I looked like a wild derby queen in pink and purple as I flew through the neighborhood. One day KJ was with me. I was wearing my favorite rollerblading outfit, a T-shirt and cutoff jean shorts that were frayed at the hem and fell sort of mid-thigh, not even close to the short shorts that some of the other girls wore.

I was self-conscious about my body. I was curvy for my age, and my brothers taunted me by calling me "big butt." I developed hips and thighs early on, and I hated it. I felt like I could never wear the types of things that other girls were wearing, because they never fit me the way I wanted. I didn't want the cellulite on my thighs to show. That was all I saw when I looked in the mirror, and I was sure that was all everyone else saw, too.

Except for KJ. As we caught our breath on a curb, he sat across from me and touched me. First his hand was on my knee. Then it moved up to my thighs. And as he slowly continued to move his hand up my leg, he said, "You're so hairy."

As with any body-conscious young woman, the smallest comment always had the biggest, longest-lasting effect on me, and later on I found myself locked in my bathroom, shaving the baby blonde hair from my legs and the more tender area farther up. KJ probably never again thought about the remark he made to me. Why would he? I was smooth from then on.

But it made a deep and lasting impression on me and left me feeling at this terribly vulnerable time in my life that I was somehow unacceptable and undesirable and needed to change myself, even this most intimate, personal area, in order to be better and more desirable, as if I even knew what that meant.

What I did know, though, was KJ gave me attention and I was willing to do anything I could to get it.

At home, the loudest voices at the dinner table were those that got heard, and I remember many times when my brothers and parents were talking and I wanted to add something to the conversation. But every time I tried to interject a comment, my voice felt too small and went unheard. Only after I gave up did someone finally ask, "What is it, Mena?"

By then, I was done and shook my head, defeated.

"Nothing," I said.

But KJ was always interested in me. Even if he was mostly interested in my body, I told myself that was okay. That was still me and it was better than being ignored.

I don't know where KJ's parents were this one day when we were at his house making out on the living room couch, like we had done many times previously. As always, he played with me and took it as far as we had gone before and then a little bit further. By this point, he had gone down on me, more interested, I think, in satisfying his own curiosity than pleasing me. I had not reciprocated, which he'd seemed okay with up until now. This time he sat back on the ottoman and pulled out a condom.

"I don't want to do that," I said, fearfully but with unmistakable clarity.

I don't want to do that.

I was fine to continue what we were doing, but not *that*, not all the way, not yet. I was about a month shy of my thirteenth birthday and didn't feel ready for *that*. KJ put the condom away, with a dejected "Okay," and I was relieved. I had been clear, and it seemed that he had understood and could be trusted to respect that limit. He had pledged his love to me for most of the year, so why would I think otherwise?

After making out a little longer, he persuaded me to follow him up to the guest room above their garage. He wanted to get out of the living room to someplace more private. The guest room was large enough for a bed and a bathroom, like a hotel room. I agreed, thinking we were going to continue what we had been doing in the house, with the same understanding. However, after a few minutes of kissing on the bed, he took out the condom again. Like before, I said no—and I said it with a tinge of fear, because I sensed something was different.

I was right, too. This time, sequestered in this small room away from the large house, with the door locked and no one likely to hear us, he didn't say okay. Instead, he kept showing me the condom, talking to me about what he wanted, and pressuring me to acquiesce, kissing me, touching me, all the while pressing his weight on top of me, until I felt trapped, suffocated, unsure of what to do, and scared, very scared.

I didn't understand why he wasn't listening to me.

Was I going to have to fight him?

Should I run?

I saw him put on the condom and felt my heart sink into a dark abyss. And just like at the dining table back home, my voice disappeared. No matter how many times I said, "No, I don't want to do that," and implored him not to do it, he didn't hear me.

I shut my eyes, and when I opened them again, KJ was climbing off me and walking into the bathroom to take off the condom.

I turned over onto my side, facing away from him, and cried.

So deeply.

So full of shame and fear.

So broken.

So absolutely terrified that I could be pregnant, because I really didn't know the first thing about sex except that I would never be the same. I wished it hadn't happened. I hadn't been ready. I was too young to even know what being ready was; I hadn't wanted to do it. And now it was too late. My virginity was gone. Stolen. The most precious part of me was taken from me by this person against my will. He had satisfied his own desire. Countless times he had professed to love me, but would he have done that against my will if he truly meant it?

I went into instant survival mode. I told myself everything was okay, that he really did love me, and maybe I . . . No, I didn't love him. And I was no longer sure he loved me. He didn't even look at me. He didn't notice my tears or hear me cry. He didn't see me curled up on the bed. How could he have seen me, though? Yes, my body was present. But the rest of me was gone, fleeing through the dark, looking for a safe place to hide, to think, to cry, to recover, to eventually shut down the emotions and tell myself that this was normal and I would be all right.

I never was all right again, because in that moment I became what I believed I had allowed to happen to me.

SLUT SHAMED

KJ took me up to that guest room above his garage a few more times. Each time, he put me on top and thrust into me while laughingly calling out, "Speed bump!" His love letters had stopped coming. In this new dynamic, he was, in fact, the only one coming and I was simply the vehicle helping that happen for him.

Then I got a bladder infection. I had never had one before, so the symptoms were strange and serious, though it's common for women to get one after having sex for the first time or even with a new sexual partner. I was taken to the doctor for remedy, and after receiving treatment for the infection, I was also given birth control pills. Medicate the physical problem, ignore the emotional scars.

I can't imagine the difference it would have made in my life if someone had asked me how I was doing and what was going on. Where had I been? Was I okay? Did something happen? Did you have sex? Are you okay with that? Let's talk about sex. Let's talk about the risks of pregnancy, what those birth control pills mean, and where you see this relationship going. All I got was a doctor writing on his prescription pad.

"Here's some medication to cure that bladder infection. And we're going to put you on birth control, too."

Welcome to womanhood.

I expected KJ to do something special for my thirteenth birthday, as well as Valentine's Day, which was the next day. It was a milestone birthday, and spending the day with me seemed appropriate and as much as I wanted and hoped for. I even missed his touch. But I found myself alone on both days. I didn't hear from him on my birthday, which was painful, and when he did see me the next day, instead of a happy Valentine's Day and an apology for missing my first day as a teenager, he said he had spent the day with a friend from high school, a girl who he had occasionally mentioned as his best friend.

Which made me what?

I didn't have to ask. After giving me Pearl Jam's new CD *Ten* as a birthday gift, KJ said, "I have something else to tell you."

"What?" I asked.

"I'm breaking up with you," he said.

I was devastated, of course. But it got worse. KJ told his friends at school that he'd been having sex with me until he got bored and dumped me. He said I was a whore. Although I was younger and attended an all-girls school downtown in Charleston, people at his school still knew me. The two of us had hung out together, and they knew my brother, who heard about what KJ was saying and came home livid and disgusted.

KJ had been his best friend, and now he didn't know what to think of him—or me. I felt bad for my brother. He and I didn't mean to hurt each other, but we did, terribly. I was hurt that I had ever met KJ and that no one had protected me from him. How many possible outcomes are there when a sixteen-year-old hangs out with a twelve-year-old? But I also didn't mean to break up their friendship, and so when he confronted me and asked if KJ was telling the truth, terrified and ashamed, I denied everything.

After school, he came into my room and stared at me, confused.

"KJ said, 'Ask her about speed bump.' What the fuck does that mean?"

To this day, I still can't wrap my head around why KJ felt it so necessary to slut shame me, especially at a school I didn't even go to. It's one disgusting thing to brag about fucking someone, but carrying it further by defaming them, by destroying their dignity and self-esteem and social presence and labeling them a whore, is another. What was he trying to prove? Was he trying to rationalize away the guilt of raping me?

For me, the easiest course of action was to move on, to survive. I didn't necessarily know how to fight. I wasn't raised to acknowledge myself and my self-worth. It was easier to compartmentalize my emotions, disassociate, and look for a new way out.

One night I was with my brothers and some friends of theirs. The wounds from the breakup were still fresh and sore, but I wanted to partake in the fun the guys were having. They were mixing up a batch of fire-aid, a combination of grape Kool-Aid and grain alcohol. I swarmed around, and after bugging them enough, they let me try it. It burned my mouth and throat and then blew my head away.

After I finished the small glass they gave me, I secretly filled up another glass and drank it down, too. Soon after I was pleading for a ride in the Viper parked in our driveway. The guy who owned it volunteered, and in a flash I was in the car and feeling the wind rush in from my passenger window as we jetted down the two-lane highway in the middle of the night. It was like I was flying, like I was flying out of my body and out of myself. Cutting through the darkness. Drunk, alongside a guy whose name I didn't even know. But what did that matter compared to the feeling of speed? Of freedom? Of abandonment? Of carelessness? Of driving out of this place and out of my mind?

THE KIDS' DIVISION

Not yet five months into my teens, my résumé read like a coming-of-age movie. Thrown in and out of every school social circle. Virginity stolen. Labeled a whore. And then modeling in New York City. That ride in the Viper was like a whirlwind trip into a machine that accelerated time.

After I finished seventh grade, I was suddenly, gratefully out of that place. At least for the summer. Every day I wore heels. I walked up and down Park Avenue attending "go-sees," modeling's equivalent of auditions. I was a natural when it came to assimilating. I could make myself into whatever was required to get the job done. You want thirteen? Fine. You want eighteen? No problem. You want twenty-three? Watch me.

I was introduced to modeling about the same time that KJ was putting his hands up my pants. A representative from the Millie Lewis agency came to Ashley Hall and promoted their modeling class. I thought it sounded fun and it was close to where we lived. In the class, we were taught how to put on makeup and take a photo. To me, it was a fun distraction. When we took our headshots, everyone at the agency marveled at how I looked like I was eighteen. The agency's owner, Victor, who was also the photographer, gave me his black leather motorcycle jacket and told me to put it on. He and his wife gushed over the results. Others marveled, too.

No one said it directly, at least as far as I recall, but with my hair swept up in a fashionable French twist and wearing a white T-shirt with faded high-waist jeans and that jacket, along with makeup and lighting, I was transformed into a pubescent Cindy Crawford. I looked eighteen but was still only twelve.

The shoot led the agency to sign me. They sent me to Hilton Head to compete in a nationwide modeling contest. I entered pretty much every category and met with reps from Ford, Elite, Wilhelmina, and all the top agencies. Some of the categories required girls to be at least thirteen years old; I was one month shy, but no one questioned me. I had such a fierce outer shell. KJ had even threatened to dump me if I did well. I guess my soul traded feelings for a career.

I was five-two at the time, hardly a competitive modeling height, but I partook nonetheless. One day I met a girl who confided that she was also twelve, but she stood six feet tall. I didn't have any of the usual advantages going for me. Even Victor sort of abandoned me after he found another girl to personally chaperone around the event who was taller, very beautiful, and closer to eighteen. While practicing our runway walks, a boy from my agency came up to me and said he overheard a girl from another agency point me out and say, "She shakes her ass too much. I'm going to wipe the floor with her."

I didn't understand how someone who had never met me could say such mean things about me and develop an instant hatred. I cried to my mother in our hotel room. However, by the end of the event I'd won nearly every category I had entered, including Best Overall Petite Model (there was a thirty-five-year-old woman in the category). Nearly every agency had requested a meeting with me, and the majority of them added that they would sign me if I grew to five-six, as Kate Moss had just hit the scene and lowered the height requirement.

I had no idea what was going on or what it meant to be a winner or what to do with all the checks I received for winning the various categories, but I did know how to wear the dress and take the picture. You need sexy? I can give you sexy.

Wilhelmina took me into their kids' division, Wee Willys, and set me up to come to New York City with my parents for the summer. We moved into the Gramercy Park Hotel, the long-term residence part in the back of the building. We had a small two-bedroom for the duration of the summer, and that was my life. Auditions were brutal. I never heard compliments. Only faults. *You're too short. You're too this. You're too that.* If I wasn't going to meetings, I hung out in the park across from the hotel.

A key was needed to get into the park. I picked mine up at the hotel's front desk and sat on a bench in the private garden, reading or watching people. Every kind of life passed in front of my eyes. I made up stories about the people. Back up in our room, I mimicked their mannerisms as snatches of overheard conversation as I regaled my mother with the stories I made up about the world that had paraded up and down the sidewalk. It was better than a movie.

I booked an Oscar de la Renta swimsuit ad. Rolled hair pouring down in waves and my curvy thirteen-year-old frame squashed into a onesie in one image and a frilly bikini in another. It was my one and only highlight of the summer. I tried not to think of it all that much and not to take it that seriously. I wished I were older and built differently. And at the end of the day, or the end of the summer, I had no idea who I was or wanted to be, which was what made modeling a perfect escape. People would tell me who they wanted me to be.

That summer was a tough one for my mother, too. I wasn't sure why, but she needed to spend much of the time in bed. My father did his best to stay with her and I was told she was bleeding. That was the extent of what was communicated to me. Now even more alone and isolated, I sat on the park bench watching life pass by and pining for the day it would include me.

The wait wasn't long. At the end of the summer, we returned to Charleston and I started eighth grade. Though I'd always been an honor student, my grades fell a bit after all of my "relationship drama," as it came to be known, but I still did well. Schoolwork was the one thing I could completely control and there wasn't much else to distract me. After the holidays, people at Wilhelmina brought up the idea of my spending the next summer in Los Angeles. If my parents were agreeable, which they were, I saw no downside.

That's an understatement. I was ready. I was chasing that feeling I had riding in the Viper. I wanted to feel the wind and enjoy the thrill of freedom.

CITY OF ANGELS

Summer arrived and we made the first of several road trips to LA. I even liked the sound of this new city: the City of Angels.

We moved into the Oakwood apartments on Barham Boulevard in an odd sliver of the city that was near Universal Studios, Griffith Park, Toluca Lake, and Runyon Canyon. It was near everything but in the middle of nowhere. To me, it was our new home for the summer, just another apartment situation, and what did I care? It was temporary. I was driven around from audition to audition, so being landlocked in god only knew where was not an issue. And since I was more often than not left to my own devices when I had free time, as was my parents' way, there was plenty of room to wander.

I took aerobics classes in a small rec room and hung out at the large pool area, a popular gathering spot for kids, parents, would-be writers and producers, grifters, and whoever else had a place at Oakwood and nowhere else to go. It was also where I was lured into what would become a familiar template of friendship based on boredom and attention from a man who was ten years older than me, which this time made him twenty-four. Other details are fuzzy. I don't even remember his name. But one day, in nothing more than my bathing suit, I followed him from the pool to his apartment, where we stretched out on his living room floor and he kissed and felt me up.

I even got another CD out of it, too—Depeche Mode's aptly named album *Violator*. Why all these introductions to men, sex, and rock and roll through these sick and twisted interactions? Where were my parents? Where were the adults, any of them? And what was I looking for? Had I really chosen from somewhere inside of me that I would trade anything that I could for any form of emotional comfort?

I walked all over the apartment complex, and then I developed a fascination with climbing the nearby mountains that cast their shadows over the Oakwood in the afternoon. I marched toward them on my own, searching for a trailhead or a path up, and then climbed with a fierce determination to reach the top, to get higher and higher, as if each ascent would take me out of this world and far away from the numbing dullness, loneliness, and empty sex that was my life at the apartment complex.

Finally, something happened. I booked a Rice-A-Roni commercial. My agency reps were ecstatic. It was a national ad, they gushed. A commercial that ran nationwide had the potential to earn big money. It also qualified me for my Screen Actors Guild, or SAG, card. I became part of the union and that was everything. My agency enthusiastically explained that it can take some actors years to book a commercial and get their union card, and as such, my parents and I should consider moving to LA permanently and giving "this thing" a try.

My parents had several conversations with the folks at Wilhelmina about this so-called opportunity, but they never fully discussed it with me. Later, they claimed they were trying to shield me from adult decisions and protect and preserve my childhood, in the hope of letting me remain a carefree kid. I felt they didn't want to acknowledge what should have been painfully obvious: that my innocence had been lost a long time ago.

I don't know what I would have said if given the chance. During career day at my school the previous year, I had selected medical research as a path that interested me, not modeling or acting. A teacher at school had actually said I wasn't very good in her theater class. Yet my parents decided to move, and I went with the flow the way I had each time we had moved previously, whether it was to St. John or South Carolina.

For me, it was a matter of dealing with the changes one step at a time. Never any hopes, considerations, or expectations. Move forward, make it work, do what's required, without asking any questions.

Make it work.

Survive.

SOMEONE'S
WATCHING

Two months passed before we left Charleston. I spent that time as a freshman at Ashley Hall, where the girl who had made my life in middle school a daily hell now wanted to "do lunch" and "get together" after seeing me on TV. Yeah, as if. I realized all those moments of catty girlish nonsense in school that I had seen on TV and in the movies were real and that who I was didn't matter to her or her friends as much as the status I bestowed on them as a model and actress. I supposed I was ready to leave them behind.

Then it was welcome to LA—sort of. My parents found an apartment in the heart of the San Fernando Valley and enrolled me in Notre Dame High School, a private, co-ed, Catholic school in Studio City. But before we settled in, they had to make one more trip back to South Carolina. I had a new manager, Glenn, an engaging man in his midthirties who we had met with several times but still barely knew, and yet my parents left me with him.

I supposed they trusted him, though I really can't speak to the way they arrived at that decision. I'm guessing they had no other options, and Glenn, wanting to be the helpful new manager, said no problem. As for me, I had no choice in the matter.

It was 1994, and I was fifteen years old, with a weeklong stay ahead of me. Glenn lived in a Spanish-style home with a pool in the backyard that had the potential to be nice if it was kept up, but it wasn't. The house was dirty and musty. I slept on the couch in his living room. Glenn spent most of the time in his bedroom with the door shut. I bought my own food and labeled each of the items with my name. They were eaten regardless.

I started my new school while there. Notre Dame required school uniforms, and I got it all wrong on the first day by wearing my skirt to the stipulated length and buttoning my blouse all the way to the top. Those were the rules, and I wanted to be good and follow the rules. Little did I know that the details of this stringent dress code didn't apply, and that there were no rules in general. I was gawked at and made to feel like the odd duck out, only to have Glenn pick me up at the end of the day and ask if I saw any cute kids who might want his business card.

Not exactly the sympathetic shoulder I would have preferred after my first day at school. But he was serious. Later that week, as I was about to get out of his car in the morning, he stopped me and handed over a stack of his business cards, instructing me to hand them out to my friends. The cute ones, he reiterated, laughing, as if it were a joke.

As soon as I walked into the school's courtyard and was out of his view, I chucked the cards into the nearest trash can.

After this poor start, the week got worse. Another of Glenn's clients, a baby-faced guy who was close to my age came around the house several times. He seemed to be doing quite well, which was impressed upon me and others who also dropped by to hang out with Glenn. One day some other kids, a bit older than me, came by the house. One of them was friends with Glenn's other client, and he was a big guy, very tall and almost twice my size. They were loud and messing with me. There was a lot of yelling. I felt threatened, and as they were leaving the big guy pushed me and I pushed back.

As I regained my balance, though, something got caught in the headphones he was wearing—perhaps a finger of mine—and the headphones snapped in half. Everything stopped and he stared at me in disbelief. I didn't mean to break the headphones. But he was furious. He ran past me into the room where I had been earlier and where my CD player and headphones were and took mine. But they weren't mine. They belonged to my brother, and I was going to be damned if anyone was going to take something from my family.

I was in Los Angeles alone and it was hard for me to be away from my family, and so, in this moment, I charged this guy, screaming as I jumped onto his back and hit him with my fists, fighting as if my life depended on it. He reeled backward and slammed me into the wall. I hit my head and fell off of him. But I attacked him again, screaming that the headphones he took from me belonged to my brother and he wasn't going to take them. After another furious round of punches from me, he threw the headphones down and left.

I had never been in a fight. For that matter, I had never fought for anything. But here I was staying with this strange man, starting a new school, in a city where I had just moved and didn't know anyone, and then this guy and his friends turned and taunted me, and even tried to take something that belonged to my family. I was on my own. I had no choice but to fight back and remain on the lookout for others who might come at me. I didn't feel like I could let my guard down or trust anyone—certainly not while I was at Glenn's house, and not afterward. I needed to stay safe if I wanted to survive.

What an introduction to Hollywood.

WHAT WAS HAPPY?

The apartment my parents found was in Burbank, on a street named Tujunga, right off of the main drag of Glenoaks Boulevard. The complex was small, with a little over twenty apartments. Wood paneled and painted baby blue. Ours was a top unit with two bedrooms and a small balcony off the living room area that overlooked the busy street below. The bedrooms were across from each other and between them was a bathroom, which was mine. My parents had their own bathroom. We had come a long way from the palatial setting of Hilltop.

I walked and walked all around Burbank. The local library down the street from my house was my escape room, the place I found solace. I spent hours there, daydreaming that I could be Alice in Wonderland for a day, venturing to some far-off land where I could meet wondrous creatures full of wisdom and insight and be happy.

I didn't fit in or relate to those around me. I had a mind whose thoughts seemed apart from everyone else. I took a disposable camera and shot photos of things that captured my mind while I wandered the town. The local coffeeshop, Ground Zero, was a favorite hangout. There I played chess with other people my age, misfits and loners like me, and I wrote in my diary while sipping tea, feeling moody and refined. I was lonely. I knew how to exist only far enough to complete the day and do what was asked of me. I felt judged, unliked, and misunderstood.

Deep down I ached to find the ingredients that would make me happy. That search caused me to look out at the world through a lens of sadness—the sad, poetic, romantic, longing teen who believed she would never find happiness again and felt so completely awkward in her body and overall being. I was a mix of confusion and desire. Desire to just be normal and happy. Why was that so hard for me? Why didn't I fit in?

At my new school, my Southern roots got me labeled "the hick." My So-Cal classmates assumed I had grown up on a farm with a tractor and chickens. I was also considered a nerd, because I was way ahead in some subjects and a quick study. And when word got out that I was acting, they wrote me off as a snob.

My bedroom was my sanctuary. Like so many teens who feel alone, isolated, alienated, and different, I shut myself in this safe and sad zone, playing music, gazing out the window, asking questions of the Universe, and opening my heart to my diary.

> I linger on and on
> Forever in the longest night

What was happy?
I didn't know it anymore.

> Page after page it goes by
> As if in a state of sadness and woe

My parents rented me an upright piano and I spent every day practicing my Chopin. I'd first heard the incredibly mesmerizing melodies of Frédéric Chopin in the apartment building where we had briefly stayed before finding our place in Burbank. I remember walking around the complex, searching for the source of the most beautiful melody I've ever heard and eventually finding a young woman sitting at an upright communal piano in an open area of the complex, playing Chopin's "Nocturne in E Flat." I was completely struck.

I approached her and stood next to the piano in awe. I had never heard anything as beautiful. It was full of every emotion I felt I had ever had and was never able to express in words, and I felt like my soul was touched through sound. As I watched the woman play, I promised myself that I would learn how to play Chopin. I would find this music and learn it.

I had goofed around on the baby grand my family had had in our home in Charleston, but I didn't really know how to play, not Chopin. His music was a whole other level of challenge. But learning how to play was only part of the story. Through his music, I fell in love with Chopin himself. Later I would have fascinations with Jim Morrison and David Bowie, but not like this. During this small window when I felt like a teenager coming of age, I connected with this composer, who had died nearly one hundred fifty years earlier, at only thirty-nine, and yet seemed to know me and the way I felt to such a degree that I believe this relationship actually saved me.

Me and my beloved Frédéric. His music guided my fingers through melodies that expressed how I felt and became the only outlet I had at the time.

I practiced every day after school. My mother and father enjoyed my playing, even if it wasn't perfect, because it brought a happiness and enjoyment to our little apartment so far away from the luxurious places we had known before. I think all of us lost ourselves in the music. It felt good to play for them and myself while my mother made dinner. The atmosphere felt like it really was a home. There was stability. And even though we never talked about what had happened to us or how any of us felt about living such a dramatically different life than before, I found it enough at the time to coexist.

Life has its ups and downs
And all we seem to notice sometimes
Are the downs.
Faith is a quality we all
Need to possess and
Believe in.

SMILE FOR THE CAMERA

needed headshots and my parents had found a photographer, Branden. He was a cool, young, hip guy and beautiful to look at. I was still fifteen, closing in on sweet sixteen, when my mother dropped me off at his house in Laurel Canyon for my photoshoot. We weren't that long into the photoshoot when I began to undress. I don't remember if Branden nudged me in that direction or if the atmosphere of soft lighting, music, and focus on me seduced me into revealing more and more of myself. It seemed this was required, desired.

The connection was clear to me. If I was going to be good enough, if I was going to succeed, if these pictures were going to make people interested in me, what better way was there than to offer up my body, my beauty, my naked self?

Branden was in his twenties and I fell for him. I fell for whatever gave me pleasure and an escape, and he was that thing. At my age, everything was amplified, too. I remember when he kissed me. The feeling lingered, a door opened, shedding light on a new path. Not long after, I became a sidekick to him and his world. He picked me up in his aging VW van. Nothing made my heart sing like the sight of him outside my high school, waiting to ferry me off to his place. We made out before even getting there.

I thought he was so gorgeous and cool and I felt so special being with him. In my diary at this time I spoke of "wanting to just be so special to someone." Like the others, he took the physical aspect of our relationship to a certain point, knowing it was too risky to actually sleep with me. But he had me in every other way that was barely legal and satisfying.

I would have gone further. I didn't care and didn't see any barriers to anything regarding age. Everything that I'd had to offer as a woman was already stolen, and so it wasn't something regarded as beautiful and precious to me anymore. Everything about my womanhood was simply a tool to get what I needed—love.

We had a ravenous attraction to each other. I remember one day driving through Laurel Canyon with him when he turned swiftly into the hills, floored the car, and screeched to a halt in a secluded turnout, as if all of life might stop if we didn't find a place where we could kiss and fondle each other. One evening, I sat on the toilet in my apartment heating a sewing needle under a flame and burning his initial, *B*, into my lower abdomen.

I was in love, desperate and devoted. Many years later I looked at that scar with confusion and regret, wishing I could have felt good enough about myself, on my own, without needing to scar my body, without already giving everything I had ever had to offer to others.

I wished I could have saved a little for me along the way.

I still wonder where those naked pictures of young me went.

WASTED

t was lunchtime at school when the bell rang and I was in the girls' bathroom with some friends, including one in particular, a girl named Jill. She
was loud and extroverted and seemingly very sure of herself, as opposed
to me, who was used to catering to what others expected and looking for an
identity.

I'd had a paper bag lunch with me, but it had ceased to be of interest
after I was handed a small plastic bottle filled with a brown-tinged liquid.
One of the girls said it was tequila. Whatever—I began to drink it. This was
Charleston on a whole new level. Not just late at night on a weekend. This
was during school. I wish I had thought of eating something. I didn't consider how I would feel after finishing my share of an entire bottle of tequila
and half a beer someone else handed me between rounds. Maybe they got a
kick out of me accepting whatever they gave me.

But I'd forgotten I had a geometry test after French class, which was next.
With the bell, lunch ended and the other girls dispersed. As I exited the
bathroom and walked into the school's courtyard, everything blurred. Like
a kaleidoscope, the world merged, and suddenly I didn't know what to do. I
made it into the building, up the stairs, and to my locker. But the dizziness
was getting worse, and quickly. I saw Mary, who'd also been with us, and
called out to her.

"Mary! I can't stand!"

She chose not to hear and then was gone.

I was fucked.

I went into my French classroom. I always loved sitting in front and being engaged. But this time I went straight to the back row. I needed to hide. I had no idea what happened that entire class. I couldn't focus and concentrated on trying to appear normal, waiting for class to end.

However, with the bell came panic. I had to go next door to geometry and take that test. I was A+ in this class; it was the only math subject where I flourished, though clearly not today. My seat was in the front row and right after I sat down, the teacher came around and plopped the test in front of me. I looked at the page and looked and looked and not a single thing on it made sense. What to do, what to do?

I decided the best thing was to simply abort mission. Something was clearly building inside me from the drinking and I knew it ultimately wasn't going to be pretty. I grabbed my test, stood up, walked to the teacher's desk, and without asking, simply laid the test down in front of him and said, "I can't do this," and then walked out of class. I managed to make it down the hall to the bathroom, where I curled up around the toilet in the handicap stall and stayed there until school was out.

My brother was waiting for me in the parking lot. He was visiting us, trying to help keep everything afloat. He got a perverse enjoyment out of driving the 1983 Fleetwood Cadillac that my parents inherited after my grandmother passed. He parked in the school's lot and blared country music while scanning the exiting throng until he saw me, at which point he'd stand up on the door frame and, with twang in his voice, yell, "Meeeeenuh! Meeeeenuh!"

I hated that car. When my parents drove me to school in the morning, I made them drop me off two blocks away. And I normally gave my brother a deadly glare in reaction to the embarrassing spectacle he created. But this time, as I walked through the gate drunk out of my mind, I needed him and I was glad he was there and not my parents, no matter the circumstance. We waited briefly for my friend Melissa. It was her birthday that day, and we had agreed to give her a ride home.

She hadn't been with me at lunch and didn't know my condition. But she found out right quick. A moment after she slid into the car, I grabbed the bag with her birthday gift I'd given her earlier in the day, ripped the gift out and threw it on the car floor, and then proceeded to vomit into the bag. At a stoplight a few minutes later, I rolled down my window and threw up again. Delirious, I wouldn't even remember dropping off Melissa or getting back home. Once there, though, I retreated into my room and literally melted onto my bed.

I can't even say if I was conscious when I heard a knock at my door. I got up, cracked it open, and saw my father.

"What did you do?" he asked.

"Nothing," I slurred.

He cocked his head to show his lack of belief and bluntly said, "You reek."

Amazingly, what followed was one of the rare loving moments we shared. When I was ready, he made me broth with rice in it while I laid on the sofa in the living room. He never yelled at me, scolded me, or even asked what happened or why. I suppose it was obvious. I got drunk at school. All I wanted was to feel better and for my brother to stop taking photos of me being sick while he cackled at my suffering. I remember giving him the finger before I dozed off into a merciful, much-needed slumber.

Soon after, one of the girls in the circle I was now roaming with had a birthday party at Disneyland. Her mother chaperoned, but we broke off and found a secluded grassy area under the tram where one of her older friends (it was always a game of who liked who) pulled out a tiny brown cigarette and said it was marijuana. Or pot. Whatever—I didn't think twice about it as I waited my turn while it was passed around, then inhaled, deeply. It was an opportunity to fit in, as well as a chance to see where it took me.

The unknown turned into someplace wonderful. As the smoke escaped my lungs and dissipated into the Universe, so, too, did my worries. I finally left my body. This wasn't drinking and feeling the weight within my body. Pot made me lighter. Lighter than I'd ever felt before. I was calm, my mind was at ease; I stepped outside myself, detached from me, and everything was beautiful and problem-free.

Thinking back upon the days when feelings shown bright all through the night. No cares, no need to worry, or lie. Just remembering flying high. Always seemed we'd fly again.
Another trip, along with another friend. Why did these days end? Why did they end?

Running and laughing from place to place. Always loved the joy present on your face. Driving on down, driving on by. Following the road underneath the sky. Floating on high, floating on by. With my friend forever, and I.

These words you heard and emotions you learned. Never can you say the untrue or deny what you once knew. The days we spent searching around the town. Were the ones which we never wanted coming down. Never ever ending and more, the feeling of flying high, forever. Upon the earth, we soar.

11/14/95

43

ANOTHER MANAGER

We quickly learned Hollywood is full of managers who should pass out warning signs instead of business cards, especially when children are in the mix.

After Glenn and a couple other flaky managers, I was signed with Iain. He was in his midthirties, exactly twenty years older than me, but he had an instant and uncanny knack for relating to me on my level and my mother on a more adult level, and for conveying to both of us, in ways we wanted to hear, a deep care and concern about my well-being and career. I don't know if I was his muse or his meal ticket, not that there was a difference.

In reality, I was both. For me, Iain was a new best friend, protector, advisor, big brother, and very soon even more. He drove a convertible sports car and had a cool apartment near Venice beach. He convinced me that stardom was around the corner, waiting for me to get there, and that he was going to get me there, soon, which seemed totally credible since he was always present in my life, always driving me someplace.

And this was a good thing to me. Soon after Iain entered the picture, my family situation started to fall apart. Communication was terrible. Money was tight. My parents, separated by so many years in age, never seemed more distant. And our living situation in that apartment had never seemed as desperate. Tension built to the point that it seemed out of nowhere when my mother suddenly moved out and left me and my seventy-something-year-old father to fend for ourselves.

I practically fell apart myself. This was a reality I didn't want any part of and couldn't believe it was my life. My memories of my father and my childhood were always so grand; as a physician he had his office in the ballroom. Yes, we had a ballroom at Hilltop, I told myself. A ballroom. Life had been grand. That was the word. *Grand* and happy. And now, after so many inconsiderate and spontaneous decisions, my mother had fled, leaving my father and me in a two-bedroom apartment and shopping at the 99-cent store.

What had happened? And why?

Years later my mother said they didn't want to "bother me with issues" and that they hoped for me to just "stay a kid."

How could they not have known that part of me was long gone?

For escape, I turned to marijuana. I had already tried it and found smoking pot put me in a relaxed state where I could escape from all the immediate shit in my life. I remember Iain driving us around town in his convertible, cruising the beach and even teaching me how to drive one weekend in the empty parking lot. I don't know how, but he was able to procure me weed, and whether or not I knew it was good for me, it was what I needed to cope and survive.

One day Iain and I were in his living room, rolling a joint, which we had done numerous times either there or in his car or at one of his buddies' places. He was clearly comfortable helping me get high and with anything else I wanted or needed, and I suppose the same came to be true of the way I felt about him, and I ended up in his bed. Trauma and the cocktail created from it is a tricky thing. I tried to deny or forget about the thing that caused it and yet kept repeating it. Once again, I'd fallen into the same beginning, middle, and end of a story wherein every situation was playing out over and over: I ended up in a sexual relationship.

Here I was again, young, vulnerable, desperate for love and affection, but so numb to myself and what was really happening.

Was my life really just unfolding with me in this dream state?

How was I now with my manager in his apartment, alone at sixteen years old, getting high, with him fucking me afterward, but yet also saying, "Don't forget to brush your hair," and asking, "Do you know your lines?"

Was this what Hollywood was?

Was this my life?

I didn't feel like I had any other options or was worthy of a life any different, and when feeling that way, defeated, it's easy to coalesce with someone.

One day, after Iain had had sex with me, I took a shower, and I'll never forget seeing him in the doorway, watching me the entire time. He even commented, "Wow, you wash every part of yourself." I guess I always was a thorough girl, no matter what I was involved in.

Or maybe I was trying to scrub off my life.

HOLLYWEED

never had a curfew and had barely just gotten a pager, so my whereabouts weren't easily established. I wasn't required to give them. Nor were they frequently sought.

As my junior year of high school neared, my best friend, Nicole, moved to Providence High. Things were going fine for me at Notre Dame. The only thing that I had ever really cared about there was getting good grades, and I knew at least I had that going for me. I had always been a bookworm and enjoyed feeling engaged in learning and doing my homework. Like learning Chopin, it was one of the few things I did for myself.

However, around this time I was barely staying on top of my work, and I ended up with my math teacher telling me that I was a day late in turning in my request to take Calculus Honors and had to apply for Math Analysis instead. I had taken Pre-Calculus the year before; math was one of the subjects I was ahead in when I arrived at Notre Dame, which fueled some of the bullying, and Math Analysis was going to be a step backward.

I said no thank you. And when Nicole, who had been my best friend, said she was leaving, well, then I was leaving, too.

What's a bit ironic is that once I made it over to Providence High, I became friendly with another girl, named Gabby. She had been in the same grade as me over at Notre Dame, yet we weren't close there. It was only when we both moved over to Providence that we found a kindred spirit in each other.

Nicole was still my best friend, actually my lifeline in a lot of ways.

I literally wanted to be her. She had an older brother a grade up from us and they both exuded coolness and independence. They seemed on a different adventure than the rest of us. They lived on top of Mulholland Drive in a beautiful Spanish-style home. She drove a vintage '70s Jaguar. The two of us painted our Doc Martens, though mine had the uncool square toe that no one would be caught dead in because I'd had to buy them at Marshalls and couldn't afford the round-toe version. Nicole even had flower and butterfly tattoos on her upper thighs. She was an amazing Gemini of a soul.

I found solace in Nicole's home, in her room, and in her car when we would drive up and down from her house listening to everything that was cool and current in music, from Rage Against the Machine to the Beastie Boys and so many other artists she introduced to me. I felt safe with her. I felt like I belonged knowing that she was my friend. When everything felt stifling and small in my two-bedroom, quiet, and lonely apartment, I went to her house, where I sat in the backyard staring up at the stars and feeling the world open up.

She and her free lifestyle provided me with an outlet for questioning the Universe in whatever wild, freaky way I wanted. I could draw and paint butterflies while getting high. I wasn't escaping my life as much as trying to re-create it in a more palatable manner.

Gabby made me feel this same way, and even more so. She lived down the street from me and had a similar home situation. Things weren't easy for her there, and we connected on that. Once I was old enough to drive, my parents came up with twenty-six hundred dollars to buy me a car, a canary-yellow 1964 Ford Galaxie. It was the largest boat of a car I had ever seen. They bought it from the original owner without checking it mechanically, including the brake pads, which were hair thin and needed fixing right away.

But I drove that thing with skill. Its defects and deficiencies, like the lack of heat or air conditioning, faded into the fabric of daily use. The dashboard had all these old-school knobs, like those on a cigarette machine back in the day. Pulling one just opened the vent to the outside. Even the radio didn't work. The car drove and the lights turned on. But that was enough. I laid my boombox across the bucket seat and kept as many CDs there as possible. I must have listened to David Bowie's *Young Americans* album nonstop for an entire year. The ingenue bumping "Fame" from her front seat. It was typical LA without my being conscious of it.

The overlook that curves around in front of the Hollywood Sign was the place I went to escape and get high. This was long before the tour buses that travel up there now. It was even before there were any street signs in that area. It was dark, desolate, and quiet. One night I climbed that beater into the mountains with Gabby riding shotgun and we parked along a residential street to smoke. I saw a giant plume of smoke coming out of the front hood and freaked out that the car was overheating and likely to catch fire, maybe even explode.

Not even close. Gabby and I realized the air vents were open and the smoke we saw was coming from the huge rips we were taking from my pipe. We laughed at ourselves and realized we were smoking some very good weed.

I abandoned my piano to smoke marijuana and began to write poetry instead. Those pages took on even more importance. I poured my confused, angst-ridden life onto those pages. I checked out of my life and into my fantasies, where I longed for answers to my deepest and oftentimes darkest questions. The ability to express the enigma of my life kept me sane and alive. Even if it didn't make sense, it was something that needed to happen, like breathing. Nicole, Gabby, weed, Iain . . . work . . . my mom figuring out her own life . . . my dad aging and more incapable of managing his life . . . my soul . . . my heart . . . my sexuality . . . realizing it wasn't conversation that people wanted to have with me. It was pleasure.

This was my life and I had to deal with it.

GUATEMALA

After the Rice-A-Roni commercial earned me my SAG card, I booked several more national commercials, including one for Kodak that shot in Guatemala. I traveled there with my mother. Most of my memories of that adventure to Central America involve getting to the small town where we filmed the commercial. I listened to the Stone Temple Pilots album *Core* through headphones as we went from bus to bus with luggage piled up on top of the roof along narrow, winding mountain-side roads that had room for only one vehicle at a time.

My fear of dropping off the cliff on the outside part of the road was not unfounded, but we eventually got to our small village, where we were met by our English crew and a tutor who was supposed to school me for a specified number of hours each day but never actually got around to doing her job. Antonio, a Mexican crew member in his early twenties, helped my mother and me get settled and find our way to the set the next day. Both of us re-marked on his friendly, considerate manner—and he was cute.

I had booked the Kodak commercial by saying I was an experienced horseback rider. That was not completely untrue. Back in Charleston, my girlfriend Jennie and I had started to ride, and I had ridden a beautiful buckskin named Enrico in several competitions, including a barrel jump that we actually won. But this commercial was something else. One segment required me to ride on a horse going over a jump while I smiled into the camera. The horse they gave me, Hercules, was a magnificent creature as big as his name implied.

Unfortunately, he didn't know me and I didn't know him, and the few hours we had together were not enough time for the two of us to develop the trust and instincts needed to perform the jump as the director had mapped it on storyboards. On the day of the shoot, I was stressed. We were in a small field with an about three-foot jump set up in the middle. There was limited space on either side of the jump, a small incline leading to an area of trees on one side, and on the other a cinderblock wall with all the camera equipment smashed up against it.

Maybe twenty yards to the right of the jump was a cliff. That drop-off was what I saw when Hercules and I approached the jump, and it terrified me. But I had no other choice except to try. Several practice runs went okay. I kicked Hercules into a canter to complete the jump and then pulled him to the left as soon as we landed to avoid crashing into the camera. Then we shot a couple attempts, which we completed perfectly. But the director wasn't getting the smile that he wanted. It had to be that perfect Kodak moment.

I was so damned stressed I didn't know if I had it in me. After a few more tries, I didn't know if Hercules had it in him either. He got tired. Who could blame him? I was tired, too! The next couple takes we attempted were a bust; Hercules refused to jump. They gave me a crop and told me to whip him. Too young and inexperienced to object, I did as instructed, and after two rounds of this, Hercules had had enough. The third time I whipped him with the crop, he stopped abruptly before the jump, then lunged straight into the air and forward, which flung me out of my stirrups and sent me flying through the air.

While he galloped off, I was flat on the ground. Despite wearing a helmet, I still blacked out upon impact, and when I opened my eyes, I was in a contorted position with my arm twisted above me and everyone hovering over me, asking if I was okay. As I regained my senses, I realized I couldn't move my arm. First, I said it in a whisper and then I said it again, more alarmed, "I can't move my arm."

Production wanted to give me fifteen minutes to recover, but Antonio realized I was injured and spoke up on my behalf. Did they really think I was going to be okay in that short amount of time? And what about the horse?

He had decided he was finished. When the director asked if I was ready to try again, Antonio said he was taking me to the hospital.

At the small local clinic, Antonio spoke with the doctor and translated back to me and my mother. Without him, we would have been lost. The doctor took an X-ray of my wrist. I was surprised when the procedure took two people: the doctor who took the actual X-ray and a tech who cranked the X-ray machine to get it going. The resulting X-ray showed a hairline fracture, which needed a cast, the doctor said, but they didn't have the materials there to make one. So he wrapped my arm profusely with gauze and put it in a sling.

It was the best they could do and I would have to figure out how to cast it later. That was fine with us. At least I hadn't suffered more severe injuries.

Back at the hotel later that night, the phone in my room rang. It was Antonio, checking in on me. Rather than talk on the phone, I went to his room. We sat on his bed, talking, and pretty soon he leaned forward and kissed me. It was the same script as always—Antonio telling me how beautiful I was, how special, how good I felt, and how much he wanted me. And with my shit self-esteem always looking for some form of affection, I let it happen, this time in the hands of a man ten years older than me who did just enough to please his desires without incurring any legal ramifications, and with the young me, emotionally starved, eating it up.

After I came back from Guatemala, I did get a cast and went straight into a Pizza Hut commercial in which they hid my broken wrist. Antonio stayed in touch with me, calling every once in a while to say that he wished he could see me again.

One day, he said, wistfully.

One day, I said, having no hope it would ever happen.

GEOFF AND FRANNY

Acclaimed indie director Gregg Araki cast me in his next film, *Nowhere*. It was my movie debut, and I showed up on set so wide-eyed and unaware that when one of the producers mentioned that they thought it would be cool for the first two inches of my hair on either side of my face to be bleached, I said, "Sure, why not."

It was so typical of me. Having never been encouraged to give anything too much thought, I did what I was used to doing, what was easiest, which was to go with the flow. Move here, move there, accept, adjust, and survive. I would figure things out as needed. And I never wanted to seem like I was challenging anything. I just sacrificed whatever opinion I had in order to be liked and accepted for what anyone wanted me to be. So I became Zoe.

Zoe was cool, independent, and knew what she wanted. I guessed they cast me after seeing those traits in my spirit, and then the transformative process of acting brought them out of me. I got it. I stepped into the role as easily as I did the character's clothes and the rest was easy. I turned it on and delivered what Gregg wanted. And because he wanted it, whatever it was, it was safe for me to do, unlike in my personal life, where I was too emotionally fragile to risk expressing my true self.

During production, I became friendly with Geoff and Franny. Geoff was tall and lanky, and Franny was his smaller, feisty better half. She wore vinyl minidresses with clear Lucite Hollywood-Boulevard, fuck-me stripper heels. Geoff had met Franny years back when she'd fallen out of a high-story apartment building window; it was an absolute miracle that she didn't die.

Our friendship grew out of my infatuation. How could I hear that story and not be intrigued and want to find out more?

We bonded quickly. They seemed cool, free, and independent. They were also strangely friendly and nurturing toward me without giving off any weird vibes. I fell right in as their third wheel. I was clearly looking for a mother-father situation where I could feel comfortable and protected by older people willing to guide me and look out for my interests. And the two of them? Maybe they were purely friendly. Maybe they also needed a friend with a car, which I had. Whatever—the three of us found what we were looking for in each other.

I spent a lot of time with Geoff and Franny on and off the set. One day after work, I drove to the motel where they were living and found Franny out front, crying on the steps. When I asked why, she said Geoff was freaking out because they had run out of weed. She explained that he was an ex–heroin addict and smoking was the only thing that made him feel calm and normal. He was inside their room, screaming and yelling, and she had lost it.

I didn't have any pot to give them. Unsure of what to do, I sat with her. This was a side of their lives that I had never seen. They always had weed. They were always mellow. As I came to learn, their lives were not as stable as I imagined. Their free, hippie-like lifestyle was a tightrope walk without a safety net. Every once in a while, I found out they had suddenly moved, no warning or planning ahead of time. Then they would land someplace and surround themselves in a cloud of relaxing smoke.

I related. I was balancing a lot in my own life: a distant, broken family, a stressful and unfamiliar school situation, schoolwork, auditions, whatever sick games my molesting manager wanted to play, and now a budding success in the business that my family had bet everything on. I was pretending every single day. All I wanted to do was get high and run away from everything. Hide someplace off the dirty streets of Hollywood and smoke it all away.

I remember walking into Geoff and Franny's latest apartment off of Cahuenga Avenue in the asphalt heart of Hollywood and feeling a weight drop off my shoulders as I sat down on their sofa. They had stuffed all their shit into this two-bedroom, but it felt so homey nonetheless. Franny and I were talking and getting high when Geoff called me over to check something out. He was standing at the closed bedroom door. I walked over and he told me that this was secret, something that I wasn't really supposed to know about, but he trusted me.

Then he opened the door. Inside was a complete farm of marijuana plants growing—at least fifty plants stuck into trays growing all the way up almost to the ceiling, with lights providing the life they needed. I was shocked, stunned, amazed, and overwhelmed. It was beautiful and I didn't even care what they were doing. I never would have even understood the ramifications of such a thing at the time. I think I was more impressed that he felt like he could trust me and share a secret that big—and illegal at that!

Geoff had been an ex–body piercer and one day, as we all hung out, he cleaned my left earlobe, sterilized a needle, and stuck it in straight through, giving my ear a second piercing. It was only in that one ear, but my mother flipped out when she saw it a week or two later. She couldn't believe that I would do something like that to myself. Never mind all the other shit going on with me. But I think that was her point. Don't go advertising your problems. It was better to hide and keep them hidden where other people couldn't see them and make judgments.

The *Variety* review of *Nowhere* said the movie "conveys vividly the hyper-accentuated extremes of teen experience and the life-or-death notions peculiar to this age group. The film's tone shifts pronouncedly between comedy and drama, exultation and despair." That could have passed as a description of my life. I worked more. I thought of acting as my job, something I needed to do to get by, and I tried to communicate my willingness and reliability.

I was getting accustomed to being cast as the sexy one or the sex object, if not the disgruntled teen telling my faux family how I truly felt about my situation. It was art imitating life. I was fine with that; I wanted only to get done what needed to be done and escape back into my own little world.

I remember getting high in my trailer one day. I didn't do it often, but I did it then for some reason. On my way out, I glanced at myself in the mirror and saw not only the whole catastrophe of my teenage life that had come before, but also why my mom had pitched a fit over my pierced ear. As long as I was able to look the part, I was good.

Keep up the act. Keep fooling all of them. Including myself.

THE DAY I NEVER
EXPECTED

Shortly before my mother left, the two of us were in the car doing errands. On the way home, she detoured through the big park in Burbank, slowed down, and started telling me numerous ways my father had been horrible. Decades of resentment, anger, and hatred unfurled in a litany of complaints and criticisms that painted him as an overbearing asshole whose every decision was a bad one. I was confused, upset, shocked, and frankly, I didn't want to know any of it. I pressed myself against the door, trying to get as far away as possible, letting the wind blow in through the open window to try to muffle some of her words before they could reach me.

Why was she doing this?

My childhood had always seemed idyllic to me, especially before age nine, and she was destroying those precious memories. I had wanted to feel close to my father, to know that I was always "the apple of his eye," as he had frequently said. Though he was older by the time I was born, and well into his seventies now, I wanted to continue to believe that my parents were happy during those years when they brought me into the world. But all of a sudden I was hearing that my father was this piece of shit. I couldn't process it.

If ever there was a moment to scream *Fuck* at the top of my lungs, this was it. I went in the opposite direction. I shut my eyes, closed my ears to my mother, and pictured the past—the happier, more pleasant past.

When we had lived in the grand Rhode Island manor Hilltop, my father moved his medical practice into the large formal ballroom. It was a beautiful, palatial room. Solid wooden double doors opened up to gorgeous, segmented, floor-to-ceiling mirrors on all sides of the room. Before we moved, my father had a large, hand-carved wooden desk that sat in the middle of the room. It had always seemed to me the throne of our palace.

But by the time we trekked out to Los Angeles, all of that was lost and replaced by the small two-bedroom apartment that looked out on the heavily trafficked Tujunga Boulevard rather than the bucolic grounds of a Newport estate. My father's new office was a small wooden fold-up tray table next to his bedside, the spot where he *worked* throughout the day. Once my mother left, I couldn't tolerate the sight of my father sitting there. The visual was too much for me to handle. I checked out emotionally.

Sometimes I couldn't even bring myself to say, Hello, I'm home.

I just couldn't.

UP ALL NIGHT

We had made a trip out to visit one of my brothers in Colorado Springs. There was talk of moving my father there in an effort to take better care of him. He was too old to be left alone. It would also alleviate some of my father's financial issues. He wasn't feeble, but he was older and sedentary. I was just relieved to have this mini-reprieve from always being with him and seeing him in this state.

Just when we seemed to have come up with a plan, my brother said I needed to go to the hospital. Apparently my father had suffered a stroke. I was filled with fear as I rushed to his bedside. Once there, I looked down at him and saw he was out of it. I was at a stage in my life when I could have used a strong father to pull me from the ash can of self-destruction, yet he was in a condition where he couldn't even help himself. I thought that day might be the last time I saw him alive. In a way, it was. Though he lived until his early nineties, he recognized me less and less. Each time, I felt sadder and, selfishly, angry at the way life had treated him and was treating me.

One night I somehow found my way to a house party with a bunch of people in their twenties. Everyone was talking and the music was loud. I was sitting on the floor in the living room, a glass coffee table in front of me, and I remember noticing the carpet around me was pretty dirty, though that fleeting observation was usurped by the methodical way a guy seated next to me was cutting something up on the table.

"What is it?" I asked.

"It's the worst thing in the world," he said. "But it'll make you feel like you can do *anything*."

Sign me up, I thought. He presented it to me, and I hovered over the table and snorted it. One thick line went up my nose and my entire world shifted. Everything I had ever known or even cared about was gone. This wasn't just some marijuana. It didn't relax me and drop me into some chill vibes with these partygoers. Whatever it was I snorted put me on a whole new flight path. I was immediately trajected into a whole other universe, fast. I didn't worry about anything or start asking the little worrisome questions about my life, as pot sometimes caused me to do. It was go, go, go. My body was left behind and my mind flew.

Later that night, after I got back to the apartment where my family and I were staying, I didn't bother to unfold the couch in the living room where I was supposed to sleep. Sleep wasn't in the equation. I opened the window. I pondered the entire universe. I questioned my entire existence. And I wrote and wrote and wrote. I scribbled my life down into pages that would never be understood by anyone who hadn't entered this alternative world.

A world of meth.

With the first light of morning, I slowly returned to this reality. Knowing I hadn't slept a wink, I realized I was probably going to look like shit, and I wasn't fully aware of whether I had been as quiet as I tried to be through the night. All I knew was that I didn't want to have to explain to anyone where I been or what I had done all night. I didn't know how to explain it, either.

Oddly enough, I was grateful that I didn't know anyone in LA who did meth and that it was going to be a one-time thing. Because holy shit, it really was, as the guy said, the worst thing in the world—and way, way, way too good.

METH MONTH

Back home, I met up with Gabby one day in Burbank. She had a different group of friends from Burbank High, none of whom I had met before. I guessed things with her had changed while I was off doing the movie and hanging with Geoff and Franny, because instead of a casual let's-smoke-some-pot vibe, we ended up at one of her friends' houses and the darkness reappeared.

There it was again. I couldn't believe it. How had it found me here in LA?

Slowly but surely it became my life. And then it took over my life. The hours I was at school were spent thinking about getting out of school and doing some lines. I stayed up until late at night, slept a couple hours, then repeated the day. Before long I was pulling out my small gold lacquered butterfly embossed compact mirror and snorting a line in the school bathroom during a break. Later, I sat up all night playing eclectic indie rock on a large old-school boombox recorder Gabby had given me.

A part of meth made me hyper-aware, but there was that other part that was like the dark side of the road, and it led directly to paranoia. I spent a lot of the night waiting to hear whether anyone was going to knock on my bedroom door. While I maintained my grades, my health suffered. My entire back broke out in acne. I'd always had perfect skin. I knew it was the meth. And just like before with the birth control offered in exchange for no questions asked, I was given antibiotics to make it "go away."

Years later, when I talked to my mother about this time when she left, she said that I had told her that I hated her. Maybe I did. At the time, I felt like no one cared about me. The drugs certainly didn't help. But I hadn't wanted to hear the things she had told me about my father and I absolutely couldn't handle the situation we were currently in, so I probably did hate her for abandoning me to that situation, although I didn't want to.

I didn't want to be at home.

I didn't want to see my father the way he was at that time. I wasn't even sure who he was or had ever been.

I stayed out as much as I could. And stayed high as much as I could.

I still did everything asked of me. Schoolwork. Auditions. Sex. Only I had to know how fucked-up I was getting every day. I thought I could, and should, suffer in silence. This was obviously my fate. I prayed someone would throw me a lifeline. I was ready every single day to be rescued. It never happened.

One day I scored some shit and went back to the apartment. I sat on my carpeted bedroom floor in front of the sliding mirrored closet doors, and looked at the baggie. There was a small amount of powder in it, but it had a slight grey tinge that made me question it. Nonetheless, I cut it up, exhaled, and abruptly inhaled it into my nose. It had the burn I was pretty much used to, but as I sat there I realized it had done nothing. And I thought, *What the fuck did I just put up my nose?*

Part of me was pissed because I had spent money on this and felt cheated. Then a part of me was scared because God only knew what the hell I had just snorted. Screw it—I dumped the baggie and promised to be more careful the next time about what I purchased. That was good money going to nothing.

THE LOSS OF IT ALL

Gradually, I lost my appetite, which was convenient because we didn't have much food in the house anyway.

When we came out to California, we shopped mainly at the 99-cent store. Being the new girl at a private Catholic school where everyone lived in a house and was gifted a Mercedes for their sixteenth birthday, that was another concern of mine. I was trying not to add fuel to the fire by having people know my family took me to Marshalls and the 99-cent store. I was lucky the trends at the time turned to grunge. That was something I could afford. I also liked shopping in thrift stores. It was something to do on the weekends.

I practically lived in a pair of corduroy baby-blue elephant bell bottoms. They had the widest flare ever, completely encompassing any platform shoe I wore, and I wore very high platforms, as much stack as I could find. They dragged so much my father asked if I was "cleaning the floor." He didn't understand fashion. It was the "look."

Hyper-fueled, I got skinnier by the day. Some days all I ate was a bagel or a few handfuls of store-brand Lucky Charms.

One evening I went into the kitchen looking for whatever was in the cupboards and found a chocolate bar. Like everything else in there, it had been there a minute or two. Not much in the apartment felt like a home anymore. I unwrapped the candy bar, popped a piece in my mouth, and immediately knew something wasn't right.

I looked down at the bar and it had white stuff on it. I ran to turn on the light.

Small worms.

I gagged and scraped my tongue and washed my mouth out.

What the fuck was going on here?

I can't be here anymore.

TOTALED

moved on from spending most of my time with Geoff and Franny to hanging out mostly with Gabby. Days and nights blurred. Then I lost my best friend Nicole. Meth made it clear that life was not going to pan out. I stayed up all night, making art and listening to indie radio. I got two hours sleep, headed to school, sometimes got fucked-up in the school bathroom, and then headed home or wherever. One day I wanted to go to Nicole's, but she simply said no.

"I can't be your friend anymore," she said.

I couldn't engage. Didn't want to. Who wants to hear the truth? Instead I grew defensive and told myself that no one gave a shit about me, Nicole included. Besides that, she wasn't going to be there for me anyway, so what did I care?

Obviously I cared deeply. I just didn't know how to say it or wouldn't let myself show it, and so I swallowed the pain and disappointment in myself and life in general and moved on. That was all I knew how to do. Just keep moving on and moving forward.

Gabby was still there. We seemed to have an unspoken connection. Both of us were struggling emotionally, the wounds of broken households. Any excuse we had to leave our homes, take off for an adventure, just feel the intoxicating freedom of the wind in our faces, hair blowing, music blasting. *Where'd we come from? Don't know. Where are we going? Doesn't matter.*

I had my car. I was on my way to an audition, driving southbound down La Brea Avenue. The Galaxie always felt like a boat sailing up and down over tiny waves when I gained enough speed traveling over the slight bumps of intersection. I had my boombox on the front seat, the Doors on repeat, and just as I crossed over Fountain Avenue the wheel spun wildly in a circle. Both my hands flew off and up into the air, unsure of what the hell was happening.

I lost control of the car. The next thirty seconds or so were like an out-of-body experience as the Galaxie collided into several cars parked at meters along the passenger side, then spun around in a complete circle, landing in the gutter facing northbound, the complete opposite direction I was originally headed. It happened extremely fast, and when it stopped, I freaked out. I was okay, but the shit in my car was strewn all over the place.

I got out and realized other cars were involved in the accident. I was glassy-eyed, in shock, overwhelmed. A guy approached me, pointing to his car.

"I was on my way to sell it," he said, bewildered. "Now it's totaled."

"I'm so sorry," I said.

"And I was hit by another car before this," he added.

Someone else said that a truck that had been heading northbound just before we got there had lost a barrel of oil off the back and it slicked the entire street. I couldn't believe it; what luck. I went across the street and called my parents, hoping that they could help me. But what I cared most about and was frantic over was how I was going to get to my audition. I never made it that day. The mess was eventually sorted out, and I got a new car, a forest green Mazda 626. It was an upgrade, a family four-door with faintly modern features.

All of life was like that at the time. Cruising along, hands off the wheel, disaster, and then the relief of walking away and calling Gabby to say, "That was fucking weird."

RAVE DAZE

The rave scene was hitting hard. Gabby and her friends always seemed to be in the know about what was cool and upcoming. If she wasn't paging me with news about the latest, hottest, next thing she'd heard about, we were waiting together near a pay phone at a 7-Eleven to score and figuring out what to do after we got high to entertain and excite us. This was how I ended up at my first rave, Fungus Mungus. It was outdoors in the desert, and my mind was blown by the combination of music, drugs, and dancing under the Milky Way. Afterward, I declared, "I only do outdoor raves."

I was less picky about drugs. At the next rave Gabby and I attended, an indoor-outdoor event outside LA proper with as many different rooms as there were styles of music being played, I started experimenting with other drugs. We had procured some mushrooms, which we washed down with some Big Gulps we bought at the rave, feeling that was all we needed to guide us through the night. But Gabby said that she wanted to go find some pot. I hung back as she set out to find some. A bit later, she returned empty-handed.

"Everyone is so *mean*," she said.

Feeling disengaged and too haughty to deal with such shit, I proposed that we get the fuck out of there. So, high on shrooms, we got in my car and started the two-hour drive back to Los Angeles. The magic mushrooms made it seem like we were flying back on a magic carpet. We laughed the entire way. I credited divine intervention for us getting back safely. Driving in that condition was reckless and stupid, of course, but our hearts were full of passion for living on the edge and we believed it would get us wherever we wanted to go.

In this case, I drove us high up into the hills above Burbank, where we sat in the car talking and laughing for hours while the wind whistled through the trees. We wanted peace, we wanted relief, we wanted to feel free from this sometimes-miserable existence for as much time as we could. We were the leaders, the decision makers in our own lives. And our lives felt like they would go on forever.

A short time later, my taste in music changed and I got heavily into Deee-Lite. If I couldn't join their band, I could at least look like I was in it. I streaked my hair lilac with a temporary paste and spent hours at night putting my hair in the tiniest braids, then the next morning teasing it into a big-ass 'fro. I glued rhinestones to the tops of my barrettes and hair sprayed curled sideburns down both sides of my face for mass cuteness effect.

And then my eyes. I glittered them as much as I could. I combed through the stores on Melrose Avenue for the latest fashions, the highest platforms, and favorite designers, like Luchiny. In my baby-blue bells with little crop tops and the highest platforms I could find to give me more height, I perfected my psychedelic club kid look. Then, when Gabby mentioned the upcoming Enit music festival, which was headlined by Pornos for Pyros and Deee-Lite's lead singer, Lady Miss Kier, I was half a step ahead of her. "Done! Let's go."

By this time, my mother wasn't really in the picture and I wasn't close to my father anymore, as I didn't want to acknowledge or accept his or my current situation. So the no-curfew policy was constantly in effect and I was allowed to roam anywhere I wanted. Maybe I had such leeway because I was never arrested or in trouble. If nothing shockingly obvious wasn't manifesting on the surface, no questions were asked. I could keep on just keepin' on.

Gabby, her friends, and I drove out to Big Bear to hit Enit. I was excited to have the opportunity to be outdoors again celebrating Mother Nature and all of her wonder and glory while partying with great live music. I don't know how long we were at the festival before one of Gabby's friends sounded an alarm, announcing, "We're out of drugs." Eager for an adventure, I volunteered to "go get 'em." I had no idea where or from whom, but I trusted my instincts that I would find 'em.

It was night, and I took off up the hill to see what I could find. Once I got to the top, I wandered around, feeling high, vibe-ing, and checking out everybody around me. Then I saw this guy. He was young, tall, and skinny, and I guess I found him attractive. I walked up to him and asked if he had any pot. He had something better, he said. He showed me several small bags of powder that he said held methamphetamine—or "meth," as he said with a glint in his eye.

His name was Sean and he was several years older than me. I gave no indication that I was already familiar with this drug. After a casual, flirtatious chat, we completed a transaction. I got the drugs, and he got my phone number.

I walked back down the hill to my friends and we all got high one more time. The music was incredible, the energies were powerful, and we all slowly left our minds and our bodies that night, drifting away from the blanket we were all crammed onto until we were floating up above the pines, into the sky, and dancing among the stars.

"EVER DONE IT?"

I t wasn't long before I was spending a lot of time on the phone with Sean. Then I went out to his place on LA's Eastside. An attraction had built on the phone, and in person it was irresistible. As we were kissing and fondling each other, he took my hand and led me to the side of his house and into a carport filled with everything but a car. We sat at a table in the far corner. There he took a glass pipe out and asked me if I'd "ever done it." I didn't know what he meant by "done it," but he seemed to be referring to meth.

Since I had only ever cut it up and snorted it, I shook my head no. He flashed the devilish grin I had seen when we first met at the rave and then put a little white rock in the pipe, grabbed a lighter, and lit the outside of the bulbous pipe. I watched him take a deep hit off it, similar to a bong hit, and then he exhaled the largest plume of white smoke that I had ever seen. I'd never watched anyone do that. Grinning, he said it was way better than snorting it. He promised it would be the greatest high of my life if I wanted to try it. Though I was apprehensive, how could I resist when he offered the pipe to me? I inhaled as deeply as I could, exhaled, and almost immediately my reality shifted. I'm surprised I didn't die that day. That moment. I had never been so high in my life. I felt like my brain had melted and I lost not just my sense of self, but my whole sense of being, like I was existing before I came to be. Seeing that I had the weightlessness of an untethered balloon, Sean started making out with me, and we sat there for a minute grabbing at each other feverishly.

After a while, though, I decided that I needed to leave and got in my car to go home. For some reason, I felt the need to be in motion. My brain was caroming through multiple dimensions. I can't believe I didn't die on the freeway that day. It's a miracle I didn't kill someone else. While speeding around the loop-de-loops of the downtown interchange, I faded from one dimension into the other, my mind projecting me outward into some unknown place and then ricocheting me back to reality in just enough time for me to stay in my lane. But I missed my exit and ended up totally lost and driving for a couple hours even though it turned out I was only fifteen minutes from home.

The next time I heard from Sean, he was locked up and calling me from LA County Jail. He had been driving with a friend of his and gotten pulled over by the police. The cops searched the car and found drugs and a whole bunch of meth and guns in the trunk. Sean wanted me to know he was set to go to trial and looking at time in prison. I corresponded with him briefly and we spoke a few times over the phone. I even wrote down the info I might need for a Greyhound escape, but once he went off to jail, our lives seemed like they were going in very different directions. And the few times I later asked myself if I was that kind of girl, I shuddered from the horror of recognizing that I might have been, without realizing there were still ways my life could and would get worse.

HOLLYWOOD ACID TEST

was now actively in my Deee-Lite, "I-only-do-outdoor-raves" phase. My days moved with a frantic mix of meth and marijuana. To stay in the center of what was happening in the scene, I headed to Kandi's Kloset on Ventura Boulevard. Kandi's was the unofficial headquarters of the rave community. It sold records, mixtapes, and rave fashion. Promoters, bands, and DJs also left flyers announcing all the upcoming events. One day I walked in wearing my beloved baby-blue bells, my hair crimped with face glittered, and started looking around.

A guy who had been talking to the DJ playing records in the store walked over to me and said he wanted to give me a cool mixtape. I took it without showing much interest. Attitude was everything, and I had a ton of it when I wanted to turn it on. He said he was a lighting engineer and was working an upcoming rave called the Hollywood Acid Test. He offered me a flyer with his name and number written on it. I glanced at it and looked back up at him.

"I only do outdoor raves," I said, feeling terribly uninterested.

Later, back in my Mazda, I tossed the mixtape and the flyer into the junk pile that was my back seat. *Never*, I thought. A few nights later, though, Gabby called me sounding extremely upset. She was having trouble at home. I told her that I'd be right over. As soon as I pulled up, she ran out to the car with her father screaming behind her. I leaned over and opened the passenger door, yelling, "Get in!" Needing a destination, I remembered this was the night of the Hollywood Acid Test rave that the guy at Kandi's had told me about. Although it was nearly ten, Gabby said, "Let's go," and I headed toward North Hollywood.

I pulled into the parking lot and found a spot. We put our stuff together knowing that we'd be checked at the door for not only the payment to get in but also to see if we had any drugs or paraphernalia on us. I pulled out the baggie of meth and showed it to Gabby, as if asking what we should do with it. Only one solution came to mind.

"Let's just do all of it," I said.

We cut up a couple massive lines and did them in quick succession. Then we hurried to the entrance before the full effect kicked in. Right after paying, though, it hit me. I motioned to Gabby to follow me into the bathroom, where I wanted to compose myself before going any farther. But it was too late. I looked over at Gabby and it was obvious I didn't feel right.

"Do you have anything to eat?" I asked.

"I have a bagel," she said. "In my bag."

We stepped over to the little makeup-counter area and she propped her back up on it while she fished for the bagel in her bag and handed it to me. I sat up on the counter chewing slowly on pieces of the dry bagel as girls came in and out of the bathroom, techno music blaring and rainbow lights cascading everywhere. I missed it at first, but a girl was passed out on the bathroom floor; everyone was stepping over her to get into the stalls. I was so consumed with my soul seemingly loosening its tether to my body and the bagel being the only thing holding the connection that I sat there in awe of what was happening. I had the feeling of stepping into a 3D movie.

After a bit, and with most of the bagel ingested, we walked out of the bathroom and went over to a set of bleachers flanking the dance space. We climbed up a few rows before plopping down, and were sitting there listening to the music and watching the dancers when Gabby said, "Oh my god, the DJ is so hot!" I looked up and agreed. The DJ was hot. But my eyes continued on to the left of the stage, where I saw the guy I had spoken to at Kandi's Kloset. He was hotter.

"Oh my god, I know him!" I said.

"The DJ?"

"No, the lighting guy," I said. "He's the guy that told me about this rave."

I felt instantly cool. I knew the guy responsible for the lasers and lights that were a more beautiful version of the synapses gone haywire in our brains. I thought of the flyer that I had thrown so carelessly and disrespectfully in the back seat. Who knew? I got the urge to say hi and see if he remembered me. I tugged at Gabby's shirt and motioned for her to follow me. We snaked our way through the crowd, me in my vintage snow boots that I had glammed up with glitter puffy paint, until we were standing at the base of the stage.

A minute or two later, he spotted us in the front, acknowledged me with a friendly nod and big smile, and waved us up onto the stage. Soon we were sucking on Blow Pops and dancing above the crowd. He handed us glow sticks. I lost myself in the trails of light that moved with the sounds and beats I followed. While my new friend periodically disappeared to tend to his computer and the lights, I danced on the stage, along with Gabby, completely high out of my mind, for what seemed like hours, until the set was over.

Gabby and I were exhausted and elated from the experience and were about to move on to celebrate the rest of the night when Mr. Lighting Genius walked up to me and said he would have gotten us in for free if I had called him. I told him that we didn't know we were going to be at the rave; we hadn't planned on it.

"Totally valid. Well, I'm Tyler," he said, and then added, "I'll give you my number if you give me yours."

I thought, *Sure, why not? What's the harm?*

If only I had known I was about to give my number to the devil himself.

GOD, why did you go? Was it something I did?
Or something I said? I really don't know.
Did I treat you unfairly?
Did I treat you unkind?
Or take you for granted?

Did I demand the truth without a lie?
Please. This pain is so eternal.
Come back. Shine upon me once again.

NEVER LISTENING

My family had fallen apart. I had lost my best friend, Nicole. I was a drug addict. I didn't want to be home. And I was desperate for affection without setting a high bar when it came to who I let love me, the latest guy now on his way to prison. Desperate for affection, I was eager to latch on to anything that would satisfy those needs, and Tyler checked both boxes.

Tyler and I had been talking and hanging out more; he'd even had me over to his apartment, where we made out. I knew he was older, and something about that always felt comforting and familiar. Like, an older person must know better. They must have a better understanding of this wild world and would be able to help me through it. He was twenty-six and I was seventeen. But unlike all the older guys who took it just far enough, Tyler didn't hesitate to go all the way and then some. Eventually he sucked the soul right out of my body.

Right off the bat, though, Tyler said that he didn't mess with meth, meaning he didn't want me around if I was going to do that drug. I had come to see him once completely bent and he'd wanted nothing to do with me. He wouldn't even let me inside his apartment. He said his piece, walked back inside, and shut the door, leaving no room for debate. The next day at school I sat in one of my classes and wrote page after page on how I should be accepted for who I was and not judged by someone who didn't know me or my situation. I gave these to Tyler, hoping he would understand my need to detach after reading them.

No one had ever called me out the way he did. I was so angry. But my desire to be with Tyler was strong enough that I quit doing meth. In its place, I smoked more marijuana. I needed to continue numbing myself, and then I needed to calm my system from having been spun all the time. I listened to reggae, especially Bob Marley, and smoked as often as I could get away with it, which was mainly when I was with Tyler, because he always had some and back then good weed was scarce. It took connections to get good shit—no seeds, no stems.

Having got myself cleaner, I spent practically every day and many nights of my senior year of high school with Tyler. In that time, I came to an important and profound conclusion: with graduation, my life was going to finally begin. I compared it to being released from prison. I had never felt supported in school, whether at Notre Dame, where I had been ahead in language and math, or at Providence, where they frowned on the TV and film work I did because it caused me to miss so much class time. I was ready to be done and live my life the way I wanted. Work, smoke, hang with Tyler, smoke, listen to Bob Marley, smoke.

I think my parents were also ready for me to graduate. The tuition at these schools was a stretch for my entire family. My mother was out of the picture, my father was struggling physically and mentally. Funds had dwindled. A decade or so later I learned one of my brothers had taken out a credit card loan to pay for my senior year so I could graduate.

I drove over to Tyler's after school one day and knocked on the door. A friend of his answered but he refused to let me pass or even tell me if Tyler was there. That seemed suspicious. No matter how many different ways I tried to get information, he refused to answer. Granted, I'd shown up unexpectedly, but I had assumed that all the time Tyler and I spent together meant we were dating. I demanded to know what the fuck was going on. Why was he acting like this? Where the fuck was Tyler?

Our standoff continued for several tense minutes. Finally, he broke and said that Tyler was with some chick in the back room. Later, I found out he was fucking a stripper that he'd met the previous night. I was disgusted and pissed. I took off in a rage, speeding away from his apartment and getting on the freeway, where I drove aimlessly while screaming that he had no right to treat me like a piece of shit and I deserved so much better. I wish I had listened to myself. But I was weak and felt broken.

As much as I thought of myself as a street-smart, independent badass, I didn't know how to survive on my own. I had zero self-esteem. And so when Tyler called and called, he was able to worm his way back into my life without the slightest resistance. My life would only become trading one bad habit for another. At least now, I was off meth.

EXPIRATION DATE

One day, Tyler and I were having lunch near where he worked part-time several days a week. Apparently I had been living with him for about a year. I wasn't even aware of the anniversary until he brought it up while we ate. With the utmost casualness, he said, "You know, your year's almost up." At first, I had no idea what he meant. Then I realized that he was talking about me—and my value to him. Like with a car, he was ready to trade me in for a newer model.

Seeing that I was confused, he laughed and said he was only joking. Such brazen cruelty still didn't fully register with me, and his laughter enabled me to let it slide as a really bad attempt at humor. Survival is often based on denial. I didn't want to know what I didn't want to know. It took years before I came to see this was Tyler's way of testing the waters, of dropping a hint and manipulating my emotions in order to get something he wanted.

For the time being, though, we passed that one-year anniversary without interruption. Most days, I went on auditions. Most nights, Tyler and I went out to some music-related event—either a rave or concert he worked or to a gig where we knew someone performing. Weekends were a blaze of music, lights, and drugs. Tyler's reputation grew. He wasn't on the same level as DJs, but he was on the next rung. People complimented the way his work helped create the atmosphere. Often their praise involved gifts of drugs. People just walked up to him and gave him MDMA, liquid acid, and mescaline.

I welcomed these perks into my schedule. Tyler and I took the MDMA at the rave and then came home to smoke and chill. After taking the liquid

82

acid one night, we ended up at Jerry's Deli, where I ordered a chicken breast that I left untouched because I saw it literally pulsating on the plate in front of me. We took mescaline at Magic Mountain; on our way home, I had Tyler stop the car so I could run out and roll around on the grassy median in the middle of the roadway in order to revel in and celebrate the gorgeousness of Mother Earth.

But marijuana was always my daily drug of choice. Tyler and I smoked out on the roof of his apartment, lining up the bong with a large magnifying glass in order to light the bowl with sunlight. We called it solar bong hits, and I was convinced they were healthier because "you know, no butane." Such silliness rarely lasted longer than the flick of a Bic. Tyler had a short fuse and an explosive temper, and he took his frustrations out on me. If I didn't do something right or seemed to misunderstand him, he snapped, "What are you, a fucking retard?" Or he called me a "fucking idiot." Or a "fucking moron." Any terminology that would name my worthlessness.

At first I had no idea how to respond. Once, I tried screaming back that I "wasn't a fucking retard," which sounded absurd. Then I quit responding altogether. I don't know why I didn't just leave, but I didn't believe I had anyplace else to go. And, after a while, I wondered if he was right. Maybe I really didn't hold any value.

I felt trapped. I might have found an outlet in my mother, but I hadn't spoken to her for a long time. Only later, as with so many things, did I come to think that Tyler helped foment that disconnect by frequently referring to my mother as an idiot and telling me that she didn't give a shit what happened to me.

Deep down, I knew better. But I didn't think I had any alternatives or places to go.

My solution was to smoke more. Tyler figured it out, and one day as I opened the baggie to grab another nugg, he grabbed it and told me I needed to cool it, smoke less. It was such a mind fuck. Smoking was the way I disconnected from feeling anything. Being high made it easier. Easier to not feel triggered and fight all the time. Easier to just simply accept my situation. I was too embarrassed to tell Gabby or anyone else.

Besides, who did I have to tell? Iain? That piece of shit? Nope. My mother? She was living her best life and I never felt she really got me. My brothers? They had rescued me from bullies when we were little kids, but now they were living in different states and I didn't feel like I was emotionally close enough to them. And when I looked in the mirror? That made me feel more alone and trapped than anything else. I didn't even want to face myself, which would have meant acknowledging the drugs, the abuse, and all the other problems that I knew deep down had led me to this fucked-up situation. I was stuck—and that's why I stayed and pretended to the rest of the world and myself that this life of mine was just fine.

CHUCK

With auditions becoming constant, Iain introduced me to a new agent, Chuck, who quickly became like a brother to me.

Work had been a steady progression into more indie films and guest star roles on popular TV series, but nothing that lifted me to the next level. After I signed with Chuck, things were starting to change for the better. I also spent more time with Chuck, who took me under his wing as if I were a special project. He was that way with his clients. He had the gift of making each of us feel like we were the only one.

Once Tyler came into the picture, I'd had a hard time working with Iain. Being around him was nearly impossible and talking to him was an exercise in restraint and awkwardness. I am sure he sensed me pulling away. Tyler never knew what Iain had done with me—and to me, for that matter. Neither did Chuck, as I was too ashamed to even hint at that relationship, which required a new word or a severe modifier to describe it accurately. It took a lot of effort to make sure those emotions that had been suppressed this whole time stayed buried.

Sometimes I wondered later what my life would have been like if I had found someone to whom I could open up and spill my guts. Someone who would listen, console, help, protect, and nurture me to a healthier place. I didn't know how to talk about those things, and besides, it seemed easier and safer to keep a tight lid on them. One way to do that was to cut ties with Iain. I arranged to meet him at a café in Santa Monica, where I planned to break the news, and I took Tyler along for support.

I needed it. Once Iain got wind of my intention, he turned hostile, claiming that everything I had was only because of him, that I was nothing before he entered the picture, and all the connections and relationships with casting directors, producers, directors, and writers were because of him. His side of the exchange was ugly, petty, and gross. I thought only about the crude reality of my side: *You got what you wanted. You literally fucked me and, no thank you, I am graciously, more than I need to be, letting you know that I will no longer be in need of your "services." I'm sorry if that's difficult for you to swallow.*

When I did speak, I kept it short. For a second or two, I entertained the thought of confronting him with the truth, but I was sick of that shit and humiliated by it all and ultimately I decided it was easier to walk away. This was such a rarity for me. I didn't want to feel bad about doing something that was in my best and healthiest interest.

"ALL MY STUFF IS HERE"

'm still haunted by how my life would have been different if I had turned around and left the night when I showed up to Tyler's apartment and his best friend wouldn't open the front door more than a crack because Tyler was screwing a stripper. Instead I fought for my place inside that dump behind one of LA's landmark restaurants. Where I stayed for the next three years.

Most of my things were stuffed into a corner behind the sliding closet doors in the bedroom. A queen-size mattress was on the ground in the room's far corner. Two mismatched dressers were against another wall, and there was a small half bath. My stuff was mostly in piles on the closet floor. I spent an inordinate amount of time cleaning and straightening those small piles of my belongings, as if they were an extension of myself and that were the best self-care I could provide.

I got especially focused on them when Tyler and I fought, which we did often. I resigned myself to this tenor of relationship. It was what it was; I had to deal.

However, I would have liked respect. Tyler and I frequently bickered and fought. He treated me more like his servant than his girlfriend. I often tagged along to the raves and concerts he worked, and then he expected me to cook for him and the handful of friends and crew members he brought back at three or four in the morning. By dawn, they were going to sleep and I was left to clean up the mess. Nothing I did was good enough for him. Every task I performed was reviewed and critiqued. The belittling was constant. In retrospect, I think it was abusive. Little by little he whittled away the thin layer of self-worth I had left. I thought this was what relationships must be like, full of stress and fighting.

One afternoon I was sitting alone on the living room sofa and, in what passed for one of the rarest of my rare admissions that all was not paradise, I mused about where else I might go, before surrendering to this fate with a defeated sigh. "But I don't know. All my stuff is here."

Tyler looked at me the same way, as part of his stuff. From the start, he always made it clear that sex was an important part of our relationship. Then, after a while, it became a certain type of sex. I was pretty much always stoned, because that was just my usual day by this point, so he would try to talk me into whatever he felt was exciting to him. And anal was that thing to him.

He said he felt better. Well, not for me. But obviously that wasn't his concern. I don't think he ever asked what I wanted or what would make me feel good or happy, not in any situation and definitely not when lights were low.

I was never given the time or respect to make these decisions on my own, which is what it's like when a human being is treated like so much stuff, so I had—and to some degree continue to have—a disconnect with the shame and grief attached to such activities with my body that didn't involve my consent. The pain was real. Because even then, as Tyler tried to finish anally, I knew that besides the physical discomfort, I was not being loved. I was just a body, a receptacle for his desires, his pleasure trumping my pain, always with the awareness that someone else would say yes if I said no, and that hurt far more and far deeper than anything I endured physically.

One day I woke up in pain. When I went to the bathroom, I got scared. I saw blood. I knew of a clinic in Burbank that my mother had taken me to while I was in high school, so I made an appointment, though I was mortified when the receptionist asked why. It was even worse when I sat in a sterile examining room with my legs up in stirrups while the doctor asked questions about my sex life. I had never been so embarrassed or ashamed of myself. She poked and prodded.

Then she took a sample to test. The results came back positive for herpes. This was on top of the doctor having already told me I had a fissure. I didn't know what those were. But herpes? What was I going to do? Herpes was forever, right? I was diseased for life. Stained.

Desperate, confused, angry, alone, I turned to an aunt who once mentioned that she suffered from herpes. It was another embarrassing, difficult call to make. But she was so loving and accepting and understanding. She told me how to manage an outbreak and made me feel less alone. It was a shitty thing that happened to me, but it happened to a lot of people and they managed, and so would I. I tried hard to believe I would be okay.

Though reassured for the moment, I still had questions. I assumed that I had contracted it from Tyler. Did he know? Had he been cheating on me? Did he not use protection? It's not like I didn't think these things were a possibility. He was a nymphomaniac. A sex addict. He wanted to get laid the way I wanted to get high.

The apartment had two bedrooms. They were right next to each other. Tyler used the second one for all the computer equipment he needed to create lighting effects. It faced out on to an alley. Directly across from us and below, there was a small private gym. Once I walked into the room while he was staring out the window at a young female trainer in skimpy workout clothes and jerking off. I was shocked and disgusted. I turned and walked out without him ever noticing that I had seen him. It's amazing how quickly and firmly my coping mechanism grabbed on to denial and detachment.

Tyler was working in the second bedroom when I got off the phone with my aunt. I considered barging in and confronting him with all the questions I had and then storming out of the apartment. But just the thought of a confrontation exhausted me and made me ask what the point would be. And where would I go? I'd been down that road before. I had herpes. I believed he had transmitted it to me. But what was the point of fighting over it? I believed I loved him. And when you love someone, you accept them and sacrifice yourself to some extent, don't you?

I convinced myself to stay. It wasn't hard. All my shit was there.

I had always contributed my fair share of expenses, but Tyler talked me into covering more and more of the costs as my paychecks got bigger. Soon

I felt like I was paying for everything. Not that I objected. I'd never had a healthy relationship with money. When I had it, I was eager for everyone to join in the fun it could provide. I shared everything without asking questions. I wanted people to be happy. I also didn't want to fight.

As I drifted deeper into Tyler's dark world, I kept a lifeline to Gabby. I continued to spend time with her and her friends. One night, Gabby and our friend Atom were in my forest green four-door cruising through Hollywood. Gabby was sitting shotgun and Atom was in the back. We had just come from his place off Cahuenga and were driving southbound. I was about to make a left turn onto Hollywood Boulevard. Then, there was a crash.

It happened in a blur: the oncoming traffic lanes were clean and I looked in the direction of my turn, but at the exact same time opposite me was a car whose driver decided to change their mind, and instead of turning left, they continued straight. We collided in the intersection. The other car struck the front of my car on the passenger side. We spun around. Gabby smacked her head into the windshield glass and then slammed backward in the seat, dazed. My airbag went off and it knocked me out for a quick second. The smell was horrendous. Smokey dust was everywhere.

I wiggled away from the air bag and got out of the car, wondering what the fuck had just happened. Atom also sprang from the car. He was holding and didn't want to be there when the cops showed up. He grabbed his backpack and walked back up Cahuenga, leaving Gabby and me to sit on the sidewalk and wait for the paramedics. Gabby needed her head checked and I had something in my eye and it hurt. We ended up going to the ER in separate ambulances and lost track of each other the rest of that night.

It turned out a piece of the airbag was lodged in my eye; a doctor flushed it out and sent me home. Gabby had a severe bump on her head. Fortunately, both of us were fine and able to resume our normal lives the next day. I always felt badly that I had put her in that situation that night. I was fine with hurting myself, just not anyone else.

Despite the near disaster, Tyler went on about his business as if nothing had happened, and eventually I did, too. He played video games, we got high, we had sex, we worked. Denial and detachment are as powerful as any tranquilizer or painkiller on the market, and just as addictive.

Soon I was sitting on the deep cushioned sectional in the living room, reading a script for a new project titled *American Pie*. I was up for the role of Heather, a sweet, innocent, virginal choir girl. I liked her because she was in the choir. Back at Ashley Hall in Charleston, I had spent three years in the school choir. At my audition, when they asked if I could sing, I said yes, and they gave me the job. Thank God they didn't ask me anything else.

MISS AMERICAN PIE

Working on *American Pie* was an experience unlike any other I'd ever had. It was strange. It was beautiful. It was fun. And more than anything else, it was normal.

I rehearsed my part as a choir girl with actor Chris Klein, who was fresh-faced, handsome, and, at twenty years old, only two years older than me. Ironically, we rehearsed in a studio down the street from the apartment where I lived with Tyler. Those rehearsals were my escape, magic time, something better than any drug I had ever taken. Instead of a high, they gave me normalcy. The opportunity to go into a fun, warm, and spirited place to sing. To joke around and be cute with someone who was my age.

And here was the thing that really spun my head. Chris was nice, kind, and well-mannered. In other words, he was a gentleman.

Oddly enough, I was always able to see those special qualities in others, but I couldn't see them in myself. Worse, I couldn't see myself deserving of being with someone who possessed those qualities. I wasn't good enough. At the end of the day, I went back to my hellhole down the street, where I got high, submitted to Tyler, and prayed to God I'd wake up in the morning so I could get back to my work.

Imagine looking forward to someone asking how you are, how your night was, or just saying it's good to see you and you looked nice.

I carefully kept my two worlds separate. I was always pleasant but never personal. I couldn't imagine Chris or anyone else finding out about my life. For me, the gift of *American Pie* was being able to spend time around people who were my own age, who were nice. My character, Heather, was in a beautiful, loving, sweet, and committed relationship with her boyfriend, the fit athlete. It was all too perfect. Heather was seen. And when confronted, she rose to the occasion and spoke her mind. It was the relationship of my dreams.

When I was little, I had felt so sure, so opinionated, and so settled. Now, as a young woman, I had lost my way. I was ashamed of my life and didn't know how to explain it to myself or anyone else, were they to have asked. I didn't know how to share it. How to take responsibility or credit for how I got here. In terms of acting, I was lucky, and grateful for the reprieve that luck afforded me, but I was really a drug addict living a fucked-up and twisted life.

I tried to put that out of mind. Every day during that shoot, I left my life and stepped into a world where people were smart, polite, respectful, fun spirited, and bright and eager to have a good time. The atmosphere was exciting, soul quenching. I got to watch women like Tara Reid and Natasha Lyonne, who had been doing this much longer than me with so much more experience, and how well versed, familiar, and comfortable they were with it all.

Booking that gig also gave me a financial opportunity I'd never had before. I felt rich and did what everyone does when they come into money: I bought a truck. My new best friend at the time, Stephanie, had a Toyota 4Runner in red and I wanted the same thing, except in a different color. I went down to a Toyota dealership outside of Los Angeles and wrote a check for thirty thousand dollars. In a way, the truck was an extension of me. It was new, clean, and sparkly. I felt proud and accomplished, like *I did that*.

It was a pale champagne with a light interior, and it was my new baby, my everything. When things got really rough between me and Tyler and our fights became truly horrendous, I stormed out and took refuge in my 4Runner. I must have packed up all my shit into it a dozen times. I drove around the neighborhood without a specific destination in mind and just screamed my head off. A blood-curdling scream. I screamed and hit the steering wheel, feeling utterly helpless.

STEPH

Tyler got a regular gig creating a light show on Tuesday nights at a dance club in Hollywood. Billed as Too Much Tuesdays, it was part rave, part dance club, part psychedelic art show, and part underground hideout for people who wanted to get really high on a school night. We had gone there a few times before Tyler got the gig, and I thought it was crazy good fun. It was set in a cavernous old warehouse in the dark, little-trafficked, decidedly uncommercial, and unhip east part of Sunset Boulevard. Tyler worked out of a small space off the stage.

One particular night, when Tyler's little area became too claustrophobic for me, I wandered into the main area and ran into Stephanie, who I knew from Gregg Araki's movie *Nowhere*. Stephanie had been in the Geoff and Franny circle. She had, in fact, seen them recently in the store where she worked on Melrose Avenue, an eclectic marketplace where artisans, crafters, and designers rented booths and sold their wares.

She was launching her own fashion line and invited me to be a part of the photoshoot. The next weekend, Gabby and I spent the day at Stephanie's house, which she shared with her boyfriend, Shawn, and two cats, Sam and Tazman. We tried on the cute little skirts and crop tops that Stephanie had hand cut and patterned herself. She was really into fun and funky fabrics, matching two-piece suits, and incorporating groovy mushrooms and cute aliens into the designs. Everything was adorable.

She reminded me of my old friend Nicole and actually became like a sister to me. Because she was a little older than me, people occasionally asked if she was my mother, which she fucking hated. I thought it was hysterical. I got into the habit of stopping by her store to smoke, hang, and talk. I also dropped by her house when I needed help preparing for auditions. Pretty soon I didn't have reasons for hanging out with Stephanie and Shawn. Whenever I needed a break from Tyler or just a place to roost, I showed up. Their home and their friendship were comfortable and safe, the refuge I needed.

One night, after we had eaten dinner together, we watched some TV show and I caught myself laughing at the jokes. I was doing something most people took for granted. I was relaxing in front of the TV and enjoying myself.

For that little bit, I felt almost normal.

TOYS

As I waited for *American Pie* to start production, my days were spent going to the gym, getting high, and hanging out with Tyler. It was a lot of waiting around for an audition, a job, a friend, the night, something. Rarely Tyler. He was always there.

During the day, Tyler mostly occupied himself by playing video games after getting stoned. Then he wanted sex. I don't know when or how he did his work. Maybe creating and programming all that stuff was easy for him. I came to see the time he spent in front of his computer included watching porn, because he shared it with me in order to tell me what he thought was sexy. He liked to point out positions and styles.

I thought I was giving him what he wanted. I had sacrificed my own well-being for him. But he wanted more. He liked toys. I had never seen any damn toys. I had no idea what the fuck any of that shit was. I didn't want to know. But I didn't feel like I had a choice. Tyler and I were driving down Santa Monica Boulevard one day when he turned his truck into the parking lot behind the Pleasure Chest, a well-known purveyor of adult entertainment. The place advertises itself as the store that has been keeping West Hollywood sexy since 1980. I had never been there or heard of it.

As soon as we walked in, I was embarrassed. I had more than proved myself not prudish, but I wanted to run back out the door. I didn't understand why people needed that stuff, and I was hurt that Tyler seemed to want it. The more he talked about these things, the more he hurt my feelings. His talk of sex toys tapped into my issues of not feeling good enough. I wondered what I hadn't done for him. As I was to discover, there was more. But at that moment, when I asked why he wanted toys and hoped to get a sincere answer, he said it was a different kind of orgasm and felt great.

He flung his arm around me and cooed about why I needed to try it, what it would be like, and how amazing and life changing it would be. He said this in the section where the dildos were displayed. He liked them. And he liked them big. I thought he was getting aroused as we shopped. I had the opposite reaction. All I could think of was that he liked to end in my rear end and now he wanted to put other things in it.

If people wanted to play with toys, fine, but it should be a joint decision, something that both parties think is playful, fun, and adventurous. I did not feel like I had that option. Tyler walked out of the store with a large, veiny, fleshy dildo with some sort of suction cup attachment on its end, and said he was excited to get home and give me my present.

I feel like a part of my soul died every time I allowed him to use it. I wanted sex to be about love, not surrender and pain. I still remember the feeling as he put it inside me. A long, lingering sadness that moved through my body, draining my spirit and destroying my soul. Sadly, I started to get used to the feeling, which was like getting accustomed to a near-death experience. Then I would have enough. I'd pack my truck full of everything I owned and drive around the city, screaming, and each time Tyler would call and talk me back to the apartment, as if he were reeling me in on a fishing line.

For the next few days, Tyler would be nice and then he would go right back to the same old behavior. As much as I wanted to be treated with kindness, love, and respect, I didn't know how to exist on my own, and so I surrendered to him. I thought if I made him happy, he would reward me with tenderness and consideration. I was naive—and wrong.

On our next trip to Too Much Tuesdays, Tyler started to comment on other women. I knew of his deviant desires but hearing them escalate like this caused me to step back and try to figure out what was going on and what he had in store for me. I had seen him jerking off to a girl sitting across our alley. He had crashed his car while looking at a hot girl on the sidewalk. He had begged me to fuck him outside or while on a hike where other people might see us. He had even taken me to a strip club on amateur night and encouraged me to "get up there." I thought of him as a walking index of categories on a porn website.

Then, from the little area offstage where he was working, he pointed out a brown-skinned woman with large breasts. He was working, we were high, and the music was thumping like one of those bad porn videos he liked to watch. He kept pointing her out to me. Then he pulled me close and said he couldn't stop thinking about the three of us together.

"Go talk to her," he said. "Get her to come hang out with us."

HANDICAPPED

She was pretty. She had dark hair and, yes, very large, prominent breasts. He instructed me to follow her into the bathroom and talk to her. *Get her attention and tell her that the guy doing the lights wants to hang out. Tell her that you're my girlfriend. Tell her she can come backstage.* He seemed to know exactly what would get her attention and entice her to follow me. Who didn't want to go backstage?

I kept my eye on her and walked into the bathroom behind her. It wasn't very big, just a couple stalls all painted black to match the black tile. We couldn't help but make eye contact by the sink, and I tried to make small talk. What would she be interested in? How could I hold her attention? Maybe I could also bring up the question on whether or not she would want to get high; that was usually a sure thing.

If I hadn't been high myself, I probably wouldn't have been able to initiate this weird introduction in the girl's bathroom. I took her into the handicap stall. I chatted her up as best I could, talking about how nice she looked, and I mentioned that she should meet my boyfriend, who had created the awesome light show. He was backstage, I said, as if that last word would do the trick, which it did.

We walked side by side to the stage door and then I took her hand, flashed my backstage pass, and guided her past the security guard. I was so stoned and it all seemed too weird and wild to take the situation seriously. I had no idea how serious Tyler was. Maybe this was a game, some innocent play and flirting. It wasn't. A short time later, the three of us walked up the stairs to my and Tyler's apartment and went inside, where, as always, the first order of business was to get high—or higher, as was the case.

We sat in the living room and took some big bong rips. I studied this girl, who was very different from me. I had no trouble imagining that she could feel Tyler lusting after her. He was sitting next to me and she was directly across. The vibes were unmistakable. Did she know what was going to happen? She didn't resist when Tyler got touchy-feely with her as we made small talk. He touched her shoulder, rubbed her leg, stroked her arm. Then, when, I supposed, he felt the time was right, he kissed her.

After that, the walls came down and the clothes came off. Tyler encouraged me to kiss her. He wanted to watch. I barely knew this woman. On top of that, I had never kissed a girl before. But then I was kissing her. It all happened so fast. The kissing and then the touching, knowing that was what Tyler wanted and was enjoying. I didn't have a clue what to expect or where this was going. I wanted to make this happen for Tyler. I had no more emotion than that. I was absolutely robotic. Do this, do that. It was always the same with me, just give what was asked and put my real self aside.

Things changed when I watched Tyler kiss her. It felt like a gut punch. There are times when you can be experiencing a feeling, but then a thought enters your brain and overrides everything else, creating this space where you question yourself, what you're doing, what you're experiencing, what kind of damage you are causing. At that point, it's nothing but damage. Eventually, we were all naked and Tyler had sex with me on the couch while she watched from inches away on the floor. Then he pushed me aside and got on top of her. I immediately got nauseous. Bile burned in my stomach like a bucket full of acid.

What the fuck was happening?

I was staring at Tyler, who was enjoying himself. I thought he looked happier than he'd been in a long time. He sat on top of her chest, grabbing both of her large breasts, cupping them together, and then sticking his dick in between to fuck them. And I sat nearby, naked, holding myself for what felt like an absolute eternity. I thought he had loved me. I thought he had really felt that way only with me. What about all of the things that he had told me? Did they mean anything?

I felt the last shreds of my self-worth disappear. I believed all I had ever had going for me were my looks and the power they had over people. Now that power was gone and apparently meaningless. I was on the sofa and in second place to this woman with enormous tits. Was that the reason? How did this night turn into this nightmare? How did I enter into such complicity? And why was I allowing it to happen right in front of me?

When would it end?

Unable to control myself, I made a comment about it all, something that revealed my discomfort. Tyler slowed down and turned toward me, seemingly upset and in disbelief at the way I felt. "I fucked you first," he said, with that tone that I had heard so many times before, like he couldn't believe there was a problem.

But there was. I got emotional and started to hyperventilate. I sat there crouched on the sofa, holding my legs up together, watching him and her and this whole scenario of him on top of her and wondering how and why the fuck this was happening. And I lost it even more. But so did Tyler, for an entirely different reason.

"What the fuck? What's your fucking problem?"

In not even a minute he had completely turned the tables around so that there was an issue only because I had one. There was nothing wrong with the situation itself. Nothing wrong with him fucking this other woman in front of me other than the fact I had caused him to stop . . . well, slow down. The problem was me.

EASILY CONVINCED

Professionally, I was doing well. *American Pie* was a dream experience that poured light into my dark life. Being with the guys reminded me so much of my brothers when I was growing up. We had silly, stupid fun in and out of character. Everyone was friendly, respectful, and sweet to me, but I am sure they could tell there was a barrier around me. I never opened up like the others and was too guarded to get very close with anyone.

Feeling like I had cheated myself out of a once-in-a-lifetime experience, I loosened up on my next film. It was another ensemble piece with people my age and I didn't want to miss out on any new friendships. But I had been living such a sick and twisted life that I thought sex was the only way to show any form of affection, and so, though I was on location for only a couple weeks, I slept with three different people on the production.

Actually, because of the things Tyler said to me before I left, I showed up thinking that he wanted me to act promiscuously and use the film as an opportunity to get kinky. He made it clear that he wanted to know—and hear—all about it.

When I checked in and told him that I had become close with several of the cast and crew, including a stand-in who was a beautiful young woman with long brown hair, he encouraged me to seduce her and let him listen in. I was already programmed to please him, so I obliged. Once I had her back in my hotel room, naked in my bed, I called Tyler and described what we were doing. He even gave us directions.

This happened a few times, always with Tyler listening in on the phone. Even long distance, he made the sex about him.

While I was acting out his extreme fantasies, I was desperate for any form of love and affection and a part of me wanted to feel what it was like to receive one hundred percent of the attention in bed. I wondered what it would be like if the pleasure of such intimacy was for my benefit, not focused solely on pleasing Tyler. Was this revenge sex? Selfish sex?

One of the guys was a production assistant who had the most enormous penis I had seen in my life. When I said as much, he gave me a blank look and said, "Really? You think so?" He was so cute, so hung, and just so dumb. The fuck was okay. Quick and okay. So sad, so unfortunate getting such a great thing and it's all over so quickly. What a beautiful waste.

I finally felt like I had found the special experience I wanted just for myself when I landed in bed with my castmate, a beautiful gem of a young man. I remember thinking he was a catch, someone with whom I could imagine going long-term. We clicked right away and had a special connection. From the get-go, it was just easy, fun, and exciting to be with him. He was everything Tyler wasn't: clean-cut, handsome, fit, healthy, a gentleman, and so sweet to me.

But I just couldn't accept it. I couldn't accept that I was worthy of him and the way he made me feel. It was too lovely and beautiful and nice, and so I pushed it away. I put up my wall, brought my attitude into play, and pushed him away so that he couldn't get any closer. I told myself that I couldn't leave Tyler. In truth, I couldn't muster the courage to be true to myself and follow my heart and my dreams. I finished the film and simply returned to LA.

Back home, I stepped into the same old routine, as if I had never been away: raves, drugs, auditions, work, girls. Many years later, I worked on a film called *Spun*. In it, actress Brittany Murphy plays a character who says, "Called a bitch up here, ordered her up like a goddamned piece of pizza!" And that was my life. Tyler would get high and decide to bring a girl over. *Ordered her up like a goddamned piece of pizza.*

By this time, though, even that wasn't enough. He had introduced a new obsession: a double-ended dildo. He loved seeing that in action. When we came home from concerts, raves, or someplace else with a girl, he usually started with me and then moved on to this new person with a feverish thirst. He liked to ride it out, leaving me to watch or try to engage. It always felt empty and depraved. There was never a moment of bliss or excitement. I was there only to help get the job done. It was another form of work.

When I was in high school, I worked at a bagel shop on Riverside Drive. I was sixteen years old and wanted a normal job. I had to purchase my own uniform and learn the different items on the menu. My first paycheck came at the end of the week, and it was a shocker. I couldn't believe how little I was paid. It was very different from acting and modeling. I figured I would get used to it over time. I wanted a normal life.

But as my personal life went sour, I showed up late. The store opened at six and I was expected to be there an hour before to help prep for the morning rush. However, I was going to bed only a few hours before that. When the manager asked if I could be counted on to show up on time, I said no, I couldn't commit. I was fired immediately.

It was the only full-time job I ever had besides acting. It was hard and unglamorous, but I would occasionally think back on the interactions I had with customers, making small talk and getting thanked, and it made me wonder how my life would have been different if I had stuck with school. I loved learning. I had a strong affinity for language, math, and science. I might have made a good doctor or medical researcher. I also loved art. Acting was easy and what I'd known how to do, but I never intended to make it a career. Right after graduating, I told myself that I was going to take a year off and figure out my life. But that was when success hit.

ANGELA

Sadly, pathetically, despite having done two studio movies, I was so completely stuck in the extremely minute management of my day-to-day survival that I couldn't appreciate these successes. After getting back from location, though, I was given a new script called *American Beauty*, and when I read it I was struck by the character for whom I was going in to read, seventeen-year-old Angela Hayes. In Alan Ball's script, she is described as "strikingly beautiful, with perfect, even features, blonde hair, and a nubile young body, she's the archetypal American dream girl."

Reading further, she is revealed as a fake, an erotic metaphor for the real feelings of love and affection that are missed. Her sexy façade is a front for inexperience and insecurity. She is the last one who thinks of herself as desirable. I felt this girl in my soul. I shuddered with a chilling recognition. I completely understood her.

I wore knee-high leather boots and a miniskirt to the audition. As I signed in at the waiting area, I saw another young actor there, also waiting. Handsome, polite, nice—I said hello and we introduced ourselves to each other.

"Mena."

"Wes."

As I left the office after my audition, he was still in the waiting room. I turned back and jokingly said, "Well, see ya on the set!"

It wasn't long before I saw him again. It was for rehearsals. Both of us had booked roles, me as Angela and Wes Bentley as Ricky.

We met several times at the production office to rehearse and get to know each other. As always, I kept my guard up and turned on the personality, as I did whenever I was around other people, especially those in the entertainment industry. I was always acting, always playing some part, in lieu of sharing my real life, which was way too complicated and beyond my capability. What would have happened if I dispensed with all the protective layers? Who would people see? Who would I see?

I just couldn't imagine making everyday conversation about my life.

No one would understand.

What I did understand all too well was that my appearance gave people a certain impression of me and caused a certain reaction. I was sensitive to this from early on and learned to accommodate it into my life. I knew what to do to let people in and to keep them out. It was challenging to say the least to manage all this. It's why I got excited every time I booked a gig. It was a chance to be somewhere new and someone else, not me.

It was why I knew the role of Angela. I could take every single moment of trauma in my life that I worked to conceal and bring it to the character, letting it rise to just below the surface, where I scared myself that someone might see.

AMERICAN BEAUTY

American Beauty is a dark, momentarily darkly comic trip through the melancholy and mystery of existence as told through the lens of a man (Kevin Spacey) searching for excitement and meaning in his life and the changes his family (Annette Bening and Thora Birch) also experience as his lust for his daughter's best friend (Angela) leads him toward a tragic reckoning with the truth.

Alan Ball had packed all the promises, real and broken, of the American dream into his script, which was being handled by director Sam Mendes, and not for nothing, it was the hottest project in the business.

But I was mostly oblivious to the part of the business where buzz started and stopped. Instead, I immersed myself in the work and arrived on the set prepared, which was fortunate.

My first day of filming was a heavy-duty scene centered on me. Angela has been confronted and rejected. Crying, she runs to the stairs to console herself. I had to sit on the stairs in front of cameras and crew and get to that extremely emotional place and cry the moment Sam Mendes called, "Action!"

On any typical day in my real life I was fragile, scared, vulnerable, desperate, confused, depressed, and feeling worthless. I had so much to draw on, but I chose my father. I thought of him—his promise, his brilliance, his decline, his feebleness. I felt cheated. Cheated from any moments I would ever have with him again. How did my life go so sour? Wasn't it not that long ago that we were swinging together on the swings at a rest stop? So much pressure, all built up, over everything. Why had things turned out this way for him, for me, and for us?

I had always drawn on memories of when things were normal, or what I wanted to remember as normal: the big family, the big house, Thanksgiving dinners, Easter egg hunts, Christmas trees, the security of knowing my parents and brothers were there for me and I was part of that tightly knit unit.

In my mind, I wrapped that life up in a neat, pretty bow and kept it prominently displayed. It was my impression of what life should be, what it had once been. But no more.

That picture had started to fade. My family had been ripped apart to the point where it didn't make sense to say I had three older brothers and a mother and father. In reality, I was all alone and trying to find my way. I hadn't wanted things to turn out like this. Too many things had transpired by this point and there really wouldn't be any going back. It was dead. And so on those stairs that day, I mourned the old me and wept for my life, a life that could have been so much more.

"Thank you," Sam Mendes said afterward.

I was sure he recognized where the acting ended and real life was revealed on camera. I trusted and felt safe in front of Sam and cinematographer Conrad Hall, or "Connie," as everyone called him. Both men were sweet, caring, sensitive. Despite the extremes of my character and the vulnerability required of me, the moments of flirtation and sexual energy that bookended the tears, Sam and Connie had that special knack for understanding and creating a nurturing, nonjudgmental, creative nest and I actually had fun playing Angela.

For me, the most difficult aspect was something most people wouldn't understand or ever see, and that was my familiarity with the content. No one I worked with during the three months of that shoot ever knew. Unlike with *American Pie*, the audition process didn't include any specific questions along the lines of "Do you sing?" I had dressed the part, and though I didn't remember anyone remarking on my outfit or attitude, I knew the nuances of this character, the little things that couldn't be taught. I'd been living this life; that's what was so ironic and scary, but only in the sense I didn't want to be found out, and I think that's why the work didn't feel as pivotal for me the way it apparently did for the rest of the cast.

I was happy to be working and have a job, and Angela certainly was fun, in moments. I got to be the girl who was pathetic and condescending to me in high school. And I could flirt for years. I knew that skill.

Thora and I had the incredible opportunity of working with Paula Abdul, who had always been another idol of mine growing up. I was all about her song "Cold Hearted"! She taught the two of us the cheerleader choreography and worked closely with me on my solo. I never really considered myself the most beautiful or sexual person in the room, but I was so familiar with putting that presentation forward that I was able to move past those insecurities and do my job.

It was important for me to do the job everyone expected of me. I wanted to please and feel rewarded by the validation. I loved seeing Sam and Connie smile. I knew attention and acclaim would come my way if I was able to deliver, and that was only going to benefit me on the set and after we wrapped. That's what I told myself when things started to connect with Kevin.

Kevin played Lester Burnham, an upper-middle-class family man who is drowning in the emptiness of his expectations. His midlife crisis leads him to fall in love with his high school–aged daughter's best friend, something he knows is illicit, illegal, and not enough to reignite the passion and meaning he wants to feel again. In that sense, I had more in common with his character than Kevin or anyone else might have dared to imagine. I'm pretty sure no one would have guessed.

Recognizing he's floundering in the pits of depression and defeat, Lester muses, "In a way, I am dead already." How many times had I said that myself in my own real life? But I left that alone. On the day Kevin and I filmed the intimate scenes in the Burnham's living room where the two of them, Angela and Lester, lie together on the sofa, an odd thing happened. Between setups, Kevin took me into a small room with a bed and we laid next to each other, me facing toward him while he held me lightly.

I wondered if he had discussed this with Sam or if it was something he premeditated as a way to prepare both of us for the intimacy we needed to share or if it was a spur-of-the-moment idea inspired by the downtime we had as the crew worked. Whatever it was, it worked. Lying there with Kevin was strange and eerie but also calm and peaceful, and as for his gentle caresses, I was so used to being open and eager for affection that it felt good to just be touched. Good and warm.

I wasn't sure if Kevin was interested in me or not. My head immediately went to that place, and I didn't know how far he was going to take it or how I was going to react if he did go there. But he didn't. We just lay there, getting close and comfortable, and it was such a genius move on his part. When we shot the scene together on the sofa, I was in a whole other headspace, and in the moment when Lester caresses Angela and tells her she is beautiful and special, I believed him. I felt like he was saying those words to me. *No, Mena, you're so beautiful and precious and I don't need to do this to you. It's possible, you can have that life and live your dreams.*

If only that were true.

Do I consider myself great?
Do I think I'm kind?
Do I see myself as lovely?
Although with every evaluation I just can't find
A way to determine what's true in my mind.
Time may hold the answer for me.
I don't know.
I can't give up.
I can't.

          —tempting though . . .

               3/6/96

BREAKING FREE

"Angela, naked, floats directly above us as if in water, kicking lazily as a deluge of rose petals falls around her. Her hair fans out around her head and glows with a subtle, burnished light. She looks down at us with a smile that is all things: compassion . . . invitation . . . lust . . ."

That was the description in the script of the movie's iconic scene. We had glorious moments shooting it. Connie stood on a ladder above me, helping the crew drop petals exactly where he wanted them to land. At the end of the night, I was told to take home as many long-stemmed roses as I wanted. It was such a special scene and day, and I told myself to keep it close to my heart and remember it when the skies darkened.

Those were the days Tyler visited the set. One time he actually brought another girl. I couldn't believe it. I saw the two of them around a corner on the set and thought, *What the fuck is he doing here?* And why was he with her? And who the fuck is she? This was my work. My sanctuary. Was he trying to sabotage me? Did he honestly think nothing was wrong with this? Was I supposed to introduce her as his other girlfriend?

It was all too fucked-up.

The whole time I worked on *American Beauty* I was grinding on empty: working to perfect my part, submitting to Tyler's demands for kinky threesomes at least three or four times a week, and pretending in both cases that everything was okay. Except it wasn't. I hated being in that situation, because I cared so much about my work.

112

I didn't have a choice other than to accept his—no, *their*—presence in this sacred place of mine. I couldn't create a scene. I couldn't complain. I couldn't talk about it. It was enough that I left the set and walked into this alternate universe every single night. Into and out of. With my work and newer responsibilities being thrown my way, I didn't have the time to fight it. And I didn't know how to fight it. By this time in the production, I had probably packed all my shit into my 4Runner a dozen times, and every time Tyler got me to come back. He called until I broke.

I couldn't afford to break anymore. I felt like I was close to rock bottom and had to hold myself together enough to finish work on *American Beauty*. No one had any idea that my best acting, better than anything I poured into Angela, was taking place off-screen. I wondered if I would ever have the strength to leave Tyler.

He had done things like this before. Many times when I had an audition coming up, he picked at me until we ended up in a massive fight. It made me feel like he was trying to sabotage my work. And my work was all I really had going for myself. I directed all my energies into being professional and acting normal just so I could get in my truck at the end of the day and head home without anyone sensing the horrendous life I kept secret.

But shortly after he appeared on the set with that chick, I found myself on the lookout on set for candy for Tyler. Just like with the film I did on location, I couldn't meet a female without questioning whether or not Tyler would approve, would like her, and how I could bring her back home for him. It happened when I met Tracy, an extra on *American Beauty*. She was about my height and size with blonde hair and light eyes. After we became friendly, I invited her over to the apartment.

The night started off normally. Tracy sat with us in the living room. We had the TV turned to some weird documentary while we smoked. Tracy wasn't really into getting high, though, and that filled me with a nervousness about what was in store. There was always a period of doubt when we brought another girl home. There was a period of discovering and testing boundaries. Pot always lowered inhibitions. Then Tyler made one of his tiny moves, a finger on her shoulders, a brief touch with his hand lingering on her body.

But as soon as that happened with Tracy, she put the brakes on it. She was immediately uncomfortable and flat-out stated that wasn't why she'd come over to our apartment. She stood up and started toward the door. I wanted to die. I had always known that this wasn't who I really was or how I wanted to behave, and her discomfort and forthrightness was like a bracing wakeup. I followed her to the door, trying to explain, but Tracy wasn't into hearing it. She headed outside, needing to get someplace where she felt safe.

I followed Tracy to the door and said I would walk her to her car. Outside, with every brainwashed excuse I could come up with, I tried to tell her that she really didn't know Tyler, that he was a good guy, that he was okay, and that this situation was all okay. I was apologizing for him, but really for myself. She listened to every word, but as she opened her car door and sat behind the wheel, she turned to me, stared me straight in the eyes, dead serious, more serious than anyone in my life had been up to then, and said, "Mena, it doesn't have to be like this."

I knew that and still I didn't know what to say in response. I was still intent on trying to convince her that things weren't really the way she saw them. Except they were. She had seen things as they were and then she did something no one else had ever done. She told me the truth. And with a bluntness I couldn't miss.

I wished I could grab on to her and say, *Take me away*. I wanted to be part of the world where this shit didn't happen. I wanted to feel normal, safe, supported, and at ease. I wanted to live in a world of possibilities, not in one at the bottom of a bong hit next to a soiled mattress.

After that, the fights Tyler and I had grew nastier. I continued to carry my shit out to my truck and leave. One of those times, though, I called up Tracy and went to her house. It wasn't that long after the scene at the apartment and she became a good friend. She lived in Santa Monica. I spent the night, believing I had finally gotten away and the relationship was over. But one night didn't break the spell. After stupidly answering Tyler's persistent calls, I found myself returning to his place the next morning to unpack my stuff back onto the closet floor.

Although Tracy didn't work out, another girl did. That was just the way it went. Her name was Brooke. She was gorgeous and blonde, just the way Tyler liked, and she was really into the threesome thing, which he appreciated even more. Normally a girl was with us for only one night; about the time I would feel totally humiliated and disgraced by all kinds of objects, her time would be up and she would leave. But because Brooke was fun and kinky, Tyler wanted to hang on to her for longer.

She became part of our lives. But I had zero relationship with her. The first time I saw Tyler fuck another girl, it broke me and I never recovered from it. Everything that I had known about love and affection flew out the window. KJ had long ago taken my virginity in exchange for a CD, but Tyler had taken whatever hope was left in my heart and soul and thrown it in the dumpster. A part of me died on that sofa that night and continued to for many years afterward. There were so many girls that I can't even remember.

The irony is that Tyler got rid of Brooke because, as he said, things were getting weird with her. One day we went over to her apartment in West Hollywood and found her hiding under her bathroom sink nursing a pile of cocaine. That was one way out. I kept thinking of the thing Tracy had said to me: *It doesn't have to be like this.* I had to find my own way out.

After *American Beauty* wrapped, I flew to Minnesota to work on the film *Sugar & Spice*. I had one of the lead roles, which meant I would be away from home for a couple of months. Tyler never took interest in my career beyond the financial contributions I was able to make. He had no interest in joining me for part or all of the time I was going to be away, so I flew off with the idea, and in fact hope, that this might be the opportunity I needed to free myself from life with him. It had the aura of impossibility, but I needed this time apart to think and set in motion the wheels of change. And before change, I needed that time to settle down, calm down, and summon the strength and courage I was going to need to finally break away.

It's clear to me now that work saved my life, but back then I only sensed it. I didn't have the perspective of time. I knew this life of chaos and abuse was wearing me down. I also knew I was fortunate to have *American Pie*,

American Beauty, and now *Sugar & Spice*. Work was my outlet. It was happening at breakneck speed. I felt like my life was happening around me, not with me, not where I was in control. I was just trying to hang on. Without these jobs, I can only imagine where I would have ended up. Broken, cast off, and cast out. In *Sugar & Spice*, I played a badass named Kansas Hill. She was tough, opinionated, and unafraid to fight for what was right. I admired her. She had the strength I needed in my life away from the cameras.

It was summer of '99. I arrived in Minneapolis feeling excited and grateful to have another job and be working. *Sugar & Spice* was about a group of high school cheerleaders who rob a bank when one of them needs money after getting pregnant. It was inspired by the true story of four teenage girls in Texas who called themselves the Queens of Armed Robbery. My costars were strong, smart young women my age, and they made going to the set every day a lively, inspiring experience. Without Tyler's cold shadow, I felt present and free. I felt something else, too: my soul was coming back to life.

I know things don't change that fast, but I knew they were changing. I had my own little living space for two months, and it was wonderful. I was drug-free. I went to sleep and woke up on my own. I didn't spend the evening looking to pick up another woman and pretending to enjoy myself while feeling manipulated and degraded. And I didn't have to go to work the next day acting even when I wasn't acting. Instead, I had space for myself, which gave me the chance to do something I hadn't done since I was a little girl. I made room for her.

We were given a few days off of production for the July 4th holiday weekend. I decided to visit my family in Virginia. I had a brother there, and I hadn't seen him in years. He knew only that I was making movies, had a boyfriend in LA, and things were cool. I hadn't seen any of them for ages, and I had a nice time except for the frustration of not hearing from Tyler. I had been trying to reach him for days because my 4Runner needed to be serviced, but I kept calling without getting an answer. Was he avoiding me? Was he with someone else? Did he ever care about anything other than himself?

I was never good in moments like these. They tapped into my control issues, my need to feel like everything was in order, even if it was all shit. I became extremely anxious when I wasn't able to put everything in its place. Like now. The day I was set to fly back to Minneapolis, I tried Tyler one last time before heading to the airport. This time he answered. He said he'd been out late and was sleeping. I figured he was probably lying and had been fucking someone else. But what did I care anymore? It was all breaking down anyway.

He must have picked up on my attitude. Suddenly, I felt like he went on the attack. He didn't like the tone in my voice, he said. He wanted to know why I was yelling at him. Blah-blah-blah. I tried to explain that I was frustrated after calling him so many times without getting any response. All I wanted to know was if he took my truck in to be serviced. It was just that one thing I wanted to know, the one thing I had asked of him. The conversation grew very heated, which I didn't have time for. I had to get to the airport. I ended the call and left with my brother. Had to go back to acting.

I was sitting with my brother at the gate (this was back in the day when you could do that), waiting to return to my life, and I didn't want to leave. I liked the idea of having a protective big brother, and I didn't want to go back out into that crazy world all alone and have to figure it out and fight my battles by myself. I desperately wanted to feel solid ground under my feet, but I had no confidence. The way Tyler had always seemed to carve up little bits of me when he called me an idiot or a retard or simply an asshole had left me frail and fragile inside.

I couldn't open up and tell my brother these things, but I did mention how happy I was going back to a movie where I was wanted, and how incredible that made me feel. While talking to him, I also had an epiphany. He was a guy. He was older than me. He was asking me questions. He listened to what I had to say. He treated me with consideration, kindness, and respect. Not belittling me. But speaking nicely, thoughtfully, respectfully. *It was possible!* Except when I tried to insert Tyler into that picture, he didn't fit. Instead of asking what was wrong with that picture, I asked myself what was wrong with Tyler.

When I got back into my hotel room, I called Tyler. I wanted to at least let him know that I'd arrived there safely. He might not have cared, but I felt it was important to give him that opportunity, and maybe I needed to hear whether he did. We had left on such a bad note before I flew back to Minnesota that I didn't want to just pick up where we had left off. I wanted to try. I could never handle a fight. I also wanted to find out if he got my truck fixed. In fact, that might have been the biggest reason I called.

It turned out he hadn't taken the truck in, and he gave me the impression that he didn't intend to. It was my problem. Sparks flew, and within minutes we were engaged in a full-blown fight on the phone. Once, a while back, I had gone "banshee," as I called it, fiercely defending myself after he asked if I was a "fucking idiot." After that episode, he dropped those pet insults of his and instead said my name in a long, slow, drawn-out manner that turned it into a slur that sounded like fingernails scraping on a blackboard. He emphasized the *Me* and then pronounced the second syllable as if negating my entire existence. *Meeeeee-nah*. He said it that way after I asked him about my truck—*Meeeeee-nah*—and I cracked.

I'm done, I thought, before going full-tilt banshee and raging about his abuse and violations of my body and my dignity, my well-being, and my self-esteem. But I wasn't done. I continued. I knew I had packed up all my shit before and always come back the next day, but not this time. I had never been this firm in my commitment to leave, never this firm or clear. Finally, I paused to catch my breath and I realized Tyler wasn't listening anymore. He wasn't even on the phone. He'd hung up. I was standing by the desk in my room and I looked at the phone with disbelief. I was stunned. I couldn't believe it. I called back. Even angrier. I waited for him to answer. It just rang and rang and rang before eventually going to voicemail. I decided to leave him a message. "You know what, Tyler?" I said in a voice that was suddenly so calm and controlled it surprised even me. "I've learned a lot about myself this weekend, about who I want to be, and what I want to do with my life, and I don't want to be with you anymore."

Click. That was it. There wasn't much to say. I had to end this madness.

Moments later Tyler called back. He'd heard my message. And, still with some renouncement of myself, I answered. His words were mean, cutting, and nasty. They were intended to wound. In the past, they would have had an effect. But now I didn't feel them. I let him spew his venom uselessly. The fire that had finally lit was going to be my own guiding light no matter how faint and fragile that flame might have seemed. I could finally see my own feet on the floor.

I hung up, walked into my little living room area, and sat down on the floor. I was stunned and in shock about what had just happened. Was I really free? Was this the time it was really going to happen? As I sat there, I realized that I hadn't shed one tear—and wasn't going to. There was nothing for me to cry about except maybe all the time I had wasted, the abuse I had suffered, the hurt I had perhaps caused in others. But that was for another time.

It was over.

I was free from Tyler.

He couldn't get me. Neither could I turn around and go back.

But what next?

Since I was so careful to compartmentalize my life, few people knew how I lived and I trusted fewer still to go to the apartment and get my stuff. I called my friend Stephanie and even reached out to my mother. I had worked so hard to keep everything compartmentalized that it was embarrassing to have to expose it. It made me feel extremely vulnerable, but my survival instinct was stronger. I needed help.

I knew only I could get my dignity back, but I asked Stephanie and my mother to help get all my stuff from the apartment, including my truck. They agreed to divide and conquer. Stephanie got into the apartment and rounded up most of my belongings. My mother faced off with Tyler in the apartment's underground garage. In recalling that experience to me later, she said she felt like he might get physical with her, and while that fear may not have been justified, I always figured the vehicle was more important to him than me.

Regardless, thanks to their heroics, I was out.

And free.

Work on the film was a well-timed distraction. Since I was needed every single moment of every day, I didn't have time to reconsider my decision or even be near my phone. Ironically, too, at this time we were busy rehearsing cheer routines. So while all this drama was happening, I was in a cheerleader outfit practicing kicks and leaps and rah-rah cheers. It was like I was congratulating myself for finally running the right play.

But the damage from Tyler had been done. I just wasn't aware of the extent or strong enough to do anything about it. I was grateful to feel like I finally had a choice in the matters of my life. I could decide what I wanted to do and with whom I wanted to spend my time. The one person I wanted to get to know was me. That would turn out to be a long and winding road that brought me to a shocking realization: I didn't know how or even want to be alone.

In a way, I never would be again. All of a sudden my anonymity was blown. One day on the set, while filming an outdoor football game scene with tons of extras in the stands, I noticed people trying to get my attention. They were shouting at me and sort of cheering. "Choir Chick!" and "Heather! Heather!" I was surprised when someone asked if they could take a photo with me and another person asked for my autograph. The attention made me uncomfortable and caught me off guard. Why was this happening all of a sudden?

It turned out *American Pie* had opened in theaters across the country, including here in Minneapolis. For obvious reasons, I had no idea. The movie was instantly popular and its characters turned into a pop cultural shorthand. I was so preoccupied that I didn't feel part of the celebration. I tried to be professional and polite. What I was completely unprepared to be was the one thing I had no say over, and that was famous. It was so sudden and so fucking strange. Everyone knew me, and I didn't even know myself yet.

I had finally said the words *I don't want to be with you anymore.* My life was a literal and complete mess in Los Angeles, my things scattered in separate homes waiting for me to organize it all. I had made room for whatever might be the next chapter. And now I was being showered with all this goodness in my life. It was too much.

The Hiding Place

Do you hide among the rushes?
Do you dance among the trees?
Do you laugh out loud and hold yourself
                        with the cool breeze?

Does your heart open to all that's new?
Does the sorrow you see affect you?
Does every day that passes by teach you of
                        the future too soon?

I wish I could laugh.
I wish I could dance.
I wish for many things; just awaiting
                        the chance.

But above the rest, forever more
'Till the day awakens on earth's side
You'll find me among the rushes galore
Tilting my head in patience to hide.

                        12/12/95

ROBERT

About two weeks after I separated from Tyler, I noticed Robert. Until then, I knew him only as the movie's cinematographer-director of photography (or the DP, as the position was known). Because of the long hours we spent together on the *Sugar & Spice* set, I had spent many hours looking at him while he did the same to me. I liked his dark, moody, longer-in-the-front, '90s-style haircut. He was about five-ten and sweet. He was also flirtatious, and I certainly knew how to play that game.

I didn't know how to be alone or want to be alone, and Robert seemed ready and willing to fill that void. He was half-German and half-Turkish. I was reminded of my father's Estonian heritage and European upbringing. I was also enticed by his maturity. He was sixteen years older than me and seemed stable. Maybe my youth and vivacious spirit brought something that he needed in his heart.

I had obviously had my own share of being intimate with men older than me, but I preferred to leave that in the past. Robert and I agreed, after we had sex in his hotel room kitchen, to be as respectful as possible with the rest of the cast and crew. We hid it pretty well. But I needed to be with someone and fill the empty space around me. His companionship and hunger for me, including sex on the carpet, was good. And oh yeah, fuck you, Tyler, I'll do what I want.

Acclimating to a new relationship that didn't involve abuse was so different it almost shocked me. In fact, it did. One night Robert and I went out to the movies. At the theater, he quickly stepped ahead to open the door and let me walk through first. No one had opened the door for me like that. Ever. It was so new and unexpected that I sort of froze and glanced up at him.

"Thank you," I said, in a tone that conveyed my astonishment.

"You're welcome." He smiled.

Was this the start of a new normal that was actually normal? I hoped so. Robert was a professional. He had a career. He was polite. It seemed incredible to me, like I had done good and was going to be okay by leaving one relationship and stepping into another one without stopping to catch my breath.

As production came to an end, I knew that I had to face a lot of shit back home and I wasn't sure what to do about it. All I wanted was to be free of Tyler, but the process took such an incredible amount of energy and emotional resources that it became more work to gain my sanity and freedom than it took to put up with it. I was scared and nervous and full of uncertainty. I didn't have a place to go. My mother had my truck. My girlfriend had my belongings. And I had this new guy.

Or did I? Was it just an on-set fling? Even as we landed in LA, I didn't know. I had no solid plans for myself, never mind a new relationship. I knew Robert and I enjoyed each other's company, and that's as much progress as I had made with the thought.

At the airport, though, I was met by a car service, a perk of having a lead role, and to be cordial, I offered him a ride to his place.

He lived in Los Feliz, on the east side of the city. When we pulled up in front of the house, my jaw dropped. It was a Spanish-style house that left me breathless—and that was just the exterior. He had remodeled it not that long before working on the movie. It had almost broken him, but he overcame all the challenges and created a dream house. Seeing my reaction, he offered me a tour. We walked through the house and I marveled at all the magnificent furnishings and details.

I stopped in the living room, overcome. I had been living in a dark, dirty, stained crypt, sleeping on the ground. This was warm and beautiful. It felt like a home. I was in awe. I looked over at him and Robert was staring at me.

"Well, do you want to move in?" he asked.

I took a deep breath and looked around before making eye contact again. I blushed. "Yes."

A REPRIEVE

t was too easy and too beautiful to resist.

I didn't think any further. I didn't think about any consequences. I didn't consider how important it might be for me to find my own place to live, create a home, and experience the rite of passage into adulthood. I didn't consider that I might benefit from being by myself, where I could sit, meditate, think, listen to my heartbeat, and heal.

Believing Robert and I were in love provided a convincing argument. He was gentle with me and looked upon me so lovingly, and that felt wonderful. I was used to being called names and treated like a toy. Robert never pushed any of those things upon me. We had great sex, something I knew how to do. I'd been trained to provide pleasure to others.

But Robert was caring, passionate, loving—the opposite of Tyler. Never malicious, damaging, or disrespectful. Yet old feelings were hard for me to shed. Over the years, something strange started to happen to me during sex. As soon as I climaxed, I burst into tears and kept crying after sex. It was intense and guttural. The sobs came from the depths of my soul, the place where I had been most damaged, only I had no idea why it was happening. Most times I tried to hide it. Sometimes I couldn't, almost as if I needed to be heard, needed to allow myself to be comforted.

Robert didn't know about the things that I had gone through with Tyler, but I did have to tell him that I had herpes. When I did, I felt a piece of me fall away. It was incredibly embarrassing to bring up. And how to say it?

I have this problem . . .

I am damaged . . .
I am damaged beyond repair . . .
Please understand it's not my fault . . .

I hadn't ever wanted to be this person, or imagined it—something damaged or used.

Robert was accepting and loving and put my fears to rest. But I had other fears. I didn't know how to be intimate. I knew how to fuck and have sex and pleasure Robert, but I didn't know how to love him. Only years later did I realize that the crying I did after sex was for me; it was the breaking open of my heart to heal. The little girl who'd had her virginity stolen needed to finally be heard.

After two months together, I began to feel at ease. Robert doted on me daily. The heaviness of my life from before was replaced by a sense of potential. He was my date on the red carpet at the premiere of *American Beauty*. Afterward, the press harped on our age difference. Reporters didn't believe me when I said age wasn't a factor and I only cared about the way Robert treated me. No one dared imagine the situation I was in before.

I felt similarly about being at the *American Beauty* premiere itself. For the event at the Egyptian Theatre on Hollywood Boulevard, my agent got me a stylist who helped glam me up in a gorgeous red designer dress with sheer paneling all the way down each side of my body. I accessorized with a small velvet bag topped by roses that I had found in a vintage store in Minneapolis. I loved getting dressed up but adding my own funky flair, and that little bag did the trick.

With Robert accompanying me in his best suit, we sailed into the glitzy press event on the wave of excitement. Red carpet. Spotlight. Press. Studio executives. Reuniting with cast mates I hadn't seen for months. It was a lot. Probably too much for me to take in. My agent and lawyer met up with us. Afterward, I was showered with congratulations, as was everyone involved in the movie. The Oscar buzz started before the party ended. I couldn't comprehend it; I had never even watched the Academy Awards.

When people told me that I was lucky, I nodded. Only I was thinking about the hell hole I'd escaped, not *American Beauty* and my newfound success.

ENGAGED

Before I took off for Canada to shoot the movie *Loser* at the end of 1999, Robert and I jetted off to Europe on vacation. I was still smoking a lot of pot, mainly on the daily, so of course we had to visit Amsterdam. Robert had family in Germany, where he had also grown up, and he had extensively traveled throughout Europe, including Amsterdam. I enjoyed having a well-traveled, experienced companion. I needed that guiding hand, and it made our trip magical.

While in Amsterdam, we got engaged. I wanted to be swept off my feet and I was. Even though I was twenty and Robert was thirty-six, I didn't think about the difference in our ages except for the fact it was less than the twenty-five years that separated my mother and father. I stepped into being Robert's soon-to-be wife as if I were stepping into a new role that I was excited to play.

One of our special places was the Post Ranch Inn, off the Pacific Coast Highway up in Big Sur, California. It was and remains one of the most magical places I've been in my life. Robert and I made the drive up the coast many times. He showed me many gorgeous hideaways along the way. At the Post Ranch Inn, we stayed in one of their ocean houses that literally hung off a cliff with a spectacular view of the rocky coastline. We filled up the large bathtub and opened the windows to let cold, misty Big Sur ocean air into the bathroom. We enjoyed romantic meals at the inn's restaurant.

I felt happy and at peace there. My heart was calm and I was excited about every little thing. Life was brand-new to me, beautiful and full of promise.

Eight months later, Robert and I traveled up to the Post Ranch Inn and eloped. A designer friend made me a dress that was bohemian chic to match both my sensibility and the surroundings. We hired someone local to perform the ceremony. I smoked a big bowl before and after. Life felt better high. The shock my family and friends expressed when I called them with the news did not dampen my excitement. My days with Robert were streamlined, fun, and adventurous.

We traveled to Germany to visit his family and took side trips to Spain and Egypt. A leisurely drive from France down to the Amalfi Coast continued the fantasy. My whole world opened up and everything felt absolutely perfect. I lived without restraint or boundaries, believing anything was possible. I indulged in every whim—fashion, food, travel, luxuries—without thinking of cost. Robert's life became mine. I gave no heed to monthly credit card bills that topped forty thousand dollars.

If not working, I made art and shopped. I kept my bong in the cabinet under our bathroom sink and made multiple visits throughout the day. Robert knew about my pot habit from the beginning and tolerated it up to a point. Then one day he wanted to discuss it. He felt like my smoking took away from our relationship, "from us," as he said, and he wanted me to stop. His concern was genuine and his pain was real.

I knew he had a point. I had been living so long as a survivor and attempting to numb myself from so many problems and horrors, but maybe I didn't need to anymore. Maybe it was safe for me to come out again. I wanted to try. The two of us walked through the house, collected all my paraphernalia and weed, and threw it out.

Detox was incredibly hard. I didn't sleep and sweated through the nights. A nutritionist Robert had introduced me to helped with supplements and recommended acupuncture and homeopathy. I still found myself sitting up at night begging Robert for some weed. He sat beside me while I writhed in bed.

"Just another hit, just one," I said.

"I love you, baby," he said.

"Just one more, a little one," I pleaded.

"I love you."

I felt like I was dying. My whole body hurt and I just wanted it to stop. But after crying through it and Robert standing tough and sharing his strength, I stopped. What happened next was miraculous. I was clear and present for the first time in years. I had the time, energy, and inclination to be productive in a new way. To experience college, I took an extension class at UCLA on anatomy and physiology. I loved the routine and rigor of study. I found myself working hard not only to learn the material but also to make up for the way my grades had dropped in high school. I wanted to prove to myself that I was capable and smart enough to succeed.

I aced the class and signed up for more. I started to make jewelry and secured a business resale license that enabled me to start a little hobby business. I called it Papillon and took my pieces to boutiques around LA. Then I started making pottery. I took classes in a small arthouse with a kiln. I was remaking my life as if it were clay I could mold and shape on a potter's wheel.

The sun was always shining. My life was incredible. I lived in this magnificent home, I had a doting husband, and I was famous. The possibilities seemed endless. Life was without limits. Yet how had I arrived here? And so instantly?

I wondered if I was going to wake up and find out I was living a dream.

A BLOODY MESS

With Robert, I had everything that fuels dreams. I had an incredible home, we traveled the world, he waited on me hand and foot, and as outlandish as it sounds, he would have died for me with nary a harsh word. I know this to be true because I almost did kill him.

We were showering together, getting ready to go out to celebrate our anniversary. I was standing in front, facing Robert, who was standing in the back on the tub, and we were kidding around, playing with each other. I laughed and smacked him playfully on the chest. But I didn't realize how close I was or how quickly I smacked him, and he was caught off guard. He stumbled, placed a foot slightly on the slope of the tub, but still slipped and fell backward.

His eyes shot up to mine. He reached out his arms in an attempt to catch his fall but succeeded only in ripping open his right forearm as it crashed onto little pottery bowls filled with seashells and stones from our trips up the coast that sat on the back of the tub. Both of us jumped out of the tub, naked, with water flying everywhere. Robert grabbed a hand towel, applied pressure to his forearm, and raised it above his head. Even so, blood was everywhere.

The guesthouse that we had was off in the backyard, and his friend had been living there for some time. They had been friends long before Robert and I met and even had some personal history together, but they were platonic by now. Robert stood there opposite me, holding his arm up with the towel, blood still dripping and the towel beginning to soak through, and he told me I needed to call her. I also needed to call 911.

But I froze. I was always someone who had loved biology and anatomy and physiology. I even spoke of Zakaria Erzinçlioğlu's book *Maggots, Murder and Men: Memories and Reflections of a Forensic Entomologist* on *The Late Late Show with Craig Ferguson*. I could watch television or movies that showed operations or gory parts of nature. Yet, as Robert stood hurt in front of me, I lost it. Eventually, I called 911, but I managed only to blurt our address on repeat to the operator, who kept asking me questions and finally told me to get a grip.

An ambulance meant for us turned onto our street but was flagged down by a neighbor who all of a sudden had a massive emergency. The chances of which were incredible! The paramedics looked down the road to see Robert standing with his arm wrapped in a towel and not looking as dire as this unexpected, new patient, whom they took instead. So we waited for the next ambulance and sped to the nearest hospital. Once there, Robert refused the treatment. Though he needed immediate surgery, he didn't trust the doctors at this hospital. He had severed seven tendons in his forearm and almost severed the median nerve. It was gruesome. The pottery bowls had exploded up into his arm, leaving it mangled, and he didn't want just anyone sewing it up. He needed an expert.

In the meantime, I had called my agent, Chuck, and he showed up outside the hospital and drove us across town to UCLA, where Robert could get the expert help he needed. Chuck had become a brother and hero to me. This was proof. Robert needed to be operated on by the best surgeons in Los Angeles, and Chuck, though he had been hosting a dinner party at his house, dropped everything, told his guests to enjoy themselves, found the experts, and chauffeured us to the ER drop-off. We walked in and the nurse already knew who Robert was.

Chuck took me home and I picked up Robert a few hours later. He was operated on early the next morning. I felt guilty and gutted. How could I say I was sorry enough? I never expected anything like that would happen, and I was terrified for Robert. Remarkably, after many hours in the operating room, the surgeons were able to repair his arm, literally weaving and sewing his muscles and even his nerves back together. I thought the most remarkable thing was that he never held that moment against me.

That was love.

SIGAL

I went to Luxembourg to work on *The Musketeer*, a period film about d'Artagnan and his fellow comrades. Production continued my fantasy with costume fittings in Paris, shooting in Toulouse and other provincial cities, and overnights in five-star boutique hotels. The cast included Catherine Deneuve, Stephen Rea, and Tim Roth. On top of it all, I was making exceptionally good money. I did get very sick with a stomach virus at the start and had to be hospitalized in Luxembourg, where doctors told me I almost died, but Robert took care of me, even sleeping on the floor of my hospital room, and soon the worst was behind me.

Once recovered, I relished every day on the set. The production was magnificent, full of love and action, and an example of why people fall in love with making movies. It was work, but it felt like playtime. One of the film's producers brought two of his daughters to set, each at different times, to help produce or to step into a small role, and I befriended the one named Limor. Dark and beautiful, Limor was a bit older than me and oozed confidence and intelligence, everything I admired and wished I had now that I was sober and searching for an identity of my own.

After the film wrapped, the director invited me and Robert to his holiday party, where I met up with Limor after not seeing her for a while. There, she introduced me to her sister, Sigal, whom I hadn't seen on set in Luxembourg to meet. Like her sister, Sigal had fabulous fair skin with long black hair. Both women were gorgeous creatures. Sigal was sweet and reserved, but with an intense fire behind her eyes. She was cunning and insightful. From our first meeting, I fell captive to her alluring, mystical gaze.

She became my closest confidante, my dearest friend, my soul mate. She brought so much into my life that at one point in our relationship, I told her I wanted to "adopt [her] as my mother." She kindly told me she "didn't want the responsibility." She would be my teacher, but not my savior, she said. She would guide me, but I'd have to learn how to walk on my own two feet.

Sigal was obsessed with personal growth. She equated self-knowledge with strength. The more you know about yourself, the stronger you are, she said. As I opened up to her, she urged me to get into therapy. I had gone only once before. At sixteen, when my parents were splitting up, my mother had taken me to sit with some woman who wanted to know my most intimate details. It was too immediate, weird, and I wasn't ready. I wasn't even capable of such reflection at the time.

With Sigal paving the way, I walked into my first therapy session and sat on the sofa across from a female therapist. By way of introduction, she asked, "How are you?" and all of a sudden I burst into tears. My reaction surprised both of us. But with that simple, considerate question, something in me slammed on the brakes and I stopped running and started to let it out. I was just so exhausted.

I started seeing her once a week. Any progress I made was tempered by the painful blocks I couldn't overcome. It was too hard to verbalize some of my traumas, even to my therapist. I was also embarrassed. I told her about my family, the way it splintered, and how it left me feeling abandoned. But Tyler and the others, including my first experiences with KJ, were off-limits. Those memories were like walls that kept me from escaping. I had become too used to pretending I was okay.

One day in session, I suddenly understood that I had never allowed myself to feel badly for what had happened to me. I was so used to just "keep on keepin' on," as the saying goes, and not wanting to create any drama, so I hid it all away. I had convinced myself of any reason not to feel it. I created any excuse to flip the script; look at all the ways I was lucky.

"Obviously, things could have been worse," I told myself. "So who am I to complain?"

"You're you," my therapist said. "You're allowed to complain. You're entitled to complain. You *need* to complain. Because you didn't complain doesn't mean those things didn't happen to you. And didn't hurt you."

Sigal was right about discovering new reservoirs of strength through therapy. Over time, I told my therapist about the effects past trauma had on me, like the fact I couldn't face my husband when we had sex. I didn't know what love really was, though I thought I caught glimpses of it. Robert provided a safe space for me physically and emotionally, and he supported my efforts to grow. But I never let my guard down. Only upon climax, I broke. All the emotion pent up inside me needed to break free in a burst of tears, a twisted cocktail of confusion, shame, ecstasy, and relief.

I was trying to explain how people looked at me and thought I had it together. Even people who had known me long ago marveled at how I seemed to have pulled through and come out the other end, when in reality I hadn't come out of anything, not completely. I had just never voiced it.

I didn't know whether I had been abandoned by my family or whether I had abandoned them. The damage was nonetheless done, and there was so much I couldn't say about the lifestyle I ended up having with Tyler. The sins against my soul were too plentiful and severe to admit. Then my life changed drastically from the most toxic and abusive relationship of my life to being in two hit films and getting married at twenty-one to someone sixteen years my senior? Most people find that unrelatable.

Even I found it hard to relate to.

One day I sat in the bath and cried. I didn't feel like stopping. I mourned the loss of my childhood, the loss of my family, the loss of my innocence, the injustice I'd endured, the way I originally thought my life was going to unfold. I missed everything about my family—and being part of a family. The holidays. The birthdays. I missed me—the person I was with them and the person I might have been.

By the time I met Tyler, my mother was in Santa Monica, my father was in Colorado, and my brothers were scattered in two other states, in two different time zones. I longed for the close, comforting dynamic of childhood. Instinct had caused me to try to create that with Robert. I wanted that comfort and security, the feeling that I was loved and accepted for being me.

I cried for two days. I allowed myself to wallow in my grief and it felt extremely relieving and long overdue. I recalled a father-daughter dance my father and I attended when I was in middle school, in Charleston. It was so beautiful and fun, but I was uncomfortable that my father was also so much older. There was a joke in my family that he was older than my grandmother, and it was true. When I was seventeen, I saw him ravaged by a stroke. A part of my heart stopped beating. I remember thinking he would never walk me down the aisle. I would never have the life I had dreamed of.

Afterward, when Sigal and I were discussing our triggers and the ways others can affect us, she mentioned how therapy would change them over time.

"Something will go from bothering you for a week, to a few days to one day to a few hours, to where you finally get to a place of catching yourself and being aware and present enough to make a decision based on reason, not past emotions.

"It's about coming into your own," she added. "Trust in the process."

The bath and the two days of tears had had a cleansing effect, like a rebirth of sorts. I didn't have to hold it in any longer. I could be a victim because I had been a victim. I could also take responsibility for trying to survive.

I could be all that and more. I could move on and grow and find myself, as Sigal said. Or I could at least try.

I finally gave myself permission.

permission.

she was looking for permission.

permission to just be herself.

it hadn't seemed that it had been that long, but it had.

she had lost herself.

she wasn't sure anymore.

in fact, she never was.

she had been floating.

moving from place to place.

from moment to moment.

it was all she had known.

there was nowhere to root because the soil had never been rich enough.

but all she had longed for was a place to keep.

to stay.

to breathe.

to exist.

to meditate and marinate.

she had remembered him saying that her "year was almost up."

she had an expiration date.

time to bring in the new and get rid of the old.

it wasn't to last.

she was learning that it never would.

but she had wanted to give of herself.

purely, but explicitly.

to find the value she needed.

   only in others, but never for herself.

she became tired.

yet, consistency was the key.

she told herself that if she could hold on long enough, it would pay off.

there was a hope.

a light she could see ahead.

what she hadn't grasped was the length of the road extending beneath
  her.

the sun had kept on its path and was moving away from her.

no matter how much she chased it.

with bewilderment in her eyes, she had found herself alone.

always alone in her deepest thoughts.

void of connection and meaning.

understanding of the simplest things.

she had lost her faith in others.

faith she couldn't even remember if she'd originally had.

the time was slipping away and there was so much more she wanted to
  do.

so much she craved for, but couldn't inspire others with.

she was looking for permission.

she just needed to be enough.

SECOND THOUGHTS

Robert and I sat on the beach. We had driven up the Pacific Coast Highway. I was feeling restless, agitated. The sun was beginning to set, and as I sat with myself and my thoughts, trying to figure out how best to express to my husband what I was telling myself that I needed, and wanted, and how to say it in the most sensitive and loving way, and knowing it would be as difficult for him to understand as it was for me to articulate, it all came out wrong.

But is there any good way to say that you want more space to yourself and might need to move out without sounding like you want to break up?

"Maybe we can still stay married, but I can just get my own place?" I pondered.

Robert leaned back with eyes blinded by shock and confusion. We hadn't been married that long and I was sure he didn't expect or want to hear the words I'd just said. I didn't want to be saying them. I tried to explain I was at such odds with myself. I told him that he was responsible for so much goodness in my life. He was never physical, forceful, or demanding. He didn't demean me.

Instead, he lifted me up and supported me. He let me be as wild and weird as I wanted.

I was coming up on my twenty-fifth year of this existence. I had been sober for about four years, and I felt like I had grown and blossomed. I had worked to get closer again with my family.

I had begun to study, make art, and create a jewelry line. I was traveling the world, my work was thriving, and I was able to purchase whatever my heart desired. My life was everything compared to where and what I had come from. I was still going to therapy, and it seemed to be working. But it wasn't enough. I couldn't relate to being married at such a young age. I was hungry for life. I was restless.

I had never lived on my own. I had never established what could be mine. I sensed there was so much to my journey that I hadn't experienced yet. I was full of insecurities, questions, and unspeakable trauma that I needed to figure out.

I held Robert's hand and stroked his fingers. I hoped he could feel my love and gratitude. I reiterated how much I loved him. But I felt like I was living for someone else again, and I sensed I had to figure out who I was and learn how to love that person before I could be in a successful, sustainable, loving marriage. I didn't know if that made sense.

I had settled down with Robert at such a young age, only a month after turning twenty-one, and our relationship included expectations that I wasn't able to meet. I was aware that Robert, sixteen years older than me, was at a different place in his life than I was with mine, including his desire to start a family. We never had that conversation or any of the others involving our wants and wishes for the future. We lived together, even slept beside each other, but our lives were in different places.

The only time I allowed myself to acknowledge the truth inside me was when I caught my reflection alone in the bathroom. Or when I woke up in the middle of the night with questions swirling in my head. Did I want to build a life with Robert? Or had I let him save mine when it needed saving? Why didn't I feel like the person I was supposed to be? Did I want more? Or did I want something else? Deep down I didn't want to admit that I knew the answer.

The previous Christmas Robert bought us matching mountain bikes and we rode them through the neighborhood and up to the Griffith Observatory. Exercise agreed with me and all the energy I had. I added jogging, hiking, and yoga to my routine. Then I discovered Pilates when my jewelry-making friend Suzanne introduced me to a studio on the westside, where, upon walking in the first time, I sensed the calming aura of its healing energy. It was also where I met my new teacher, Jay.

When I had the courage to be truthful with myself, I knew he was the catalyst for the conversation I had with Robert. Jay was beautiful. He was Australian and closer to me in age. He had fair skin, dark black hair, and freckles. He was tall and fit. His body was chiseled to statue-like perfection. He was teaching Pilates while in school pursuing a degree in Chinese medicine.

A few times a week, I got in my car and drove thirty minutes to the Westside to take classes—and of course to see Jay. I wasn't conscious of what was really happening, but later I saw that every time I drove to take a Pilates class from Jay, I was gradually driving myself further away from my husband.

I loved Robert. We had a beautiful little life together, and I had flourished within it. I had discovered myself in the streets of Berlin, climbed the unfinished turrets of the Sagrada Familia in Barcelona, discovered the mysterious Giza pyramids and explored the Valley of the Kings in Egypt, where a man had asked Robert how many camels he could trade for me. We walked the narrow alleyways through Ravello on Italy's Amalfi Coast and bought cans of tuna for the stray alley cats in Rome. We bought fresh goods from the bakery in the mornings in Braunschweig and walked through the beautiful parks in the fall. We traveled everywhere. We lived, and loved, and made a home for each other, wherever we went. A Tiffany frame on our bedside held a picture from our latest adventure. Life was peaceful, prosperous, and easy.

Then one day, as I tried to explain to Robert, I knew that I had to leave it—and sadly, painfully, inexplicably, that day had come.

JAY

I got home early one day from appointments and packed a suitcase with the essentials I thought I needed to survive a week or two. I wasn't thinking in any longer term. I wanted to make the break before Robert was home. I worked with my emotions in deep check, trying to avoid feeling attached or sentimental about all the things I was leaving behind, which was practically everything. This hurried dance was clearly ad-libbed but moved through the house toward a clean escape until I got my suitcase to the front door. Then Robert walked in.

He saw my suitcase and his face reflected the range of emotions one would expect. Hoping to avoid a messy confrontation that would likely result in me turning around and unpacking, I grabbed my suitcase, stated how I needed to leave, and walked to my car without turning around.

A flame ignited inside of me that refused to be ignored despite its unsettling influence. I was very aware that I was married, but I was also aware that I wasn't happy. Although I couldn't define happy, whatever it was, it wasn't me. All I knew was that something was missing in my life. Not my life with Robert. *My life.* The life I carried around inside me.

I drove straight to Jay's. I was relieved that I had left Robert before starting anything with Jay. At the same time, I was eager to embrace him as a free woman, sure that he was going to fill the empty spaces in me with all that I craved.

It would take me much longer to understand that I was going about my life all wrong. I needed to stop constantly racing toward finding something that I thought would fit perfectly, and instead learn I could bring all the love I needed into my own life without anyone else doing it for me.

At Jay's, I literally ran inside to be with him, as if finishing the race away from my life. I hadn't told anyone about this sudden change, including my therapist. I was still avoiding the deep issues that needed to be addressed. I was still too embarrassed to admit them, and I didn't want to be judged. I was harsh enough on myself. I kept doing what I was good at, pushing forward, without seeing that I went from one extreme to the other. Either I was having an emotional breakdown and crying from the depths of my soul or I was locked away within a stone fortress that no one could penetrate. I had learned to survive by turning off my emotions, and so it was when I left Robert. I shut out his cries and his pleas and moved forward to the next thing.

As difficult as this was in the moment, I knew that I wouldn't have been a good wife to Robert. Over time I would have grown more distant, perhaps cheated on him, or made him feel stifled and stuck. I was barely twenty-one when I married him, stoned, on a cliffside in Big Sur. It was wonderful and romantic, but it was something that I could appreciate and want again only years later. I married Robert to feel safe. He took me in and took care of me. Thanks to him, I had the freedom to grow. With the love and space he provided, I was able to open up and blossom. I pushed against the limitations of the relationship, and then I needed to break free of them. I wasn't where I needed to be yet. I believed Jay was the next step in getting there.

I literally walked through Jay's front door and deposited my life in his. After gathering myself somewhat, I called Suzanne and went to her place. We sat on the sofa in her living room and I cried.

"I left Robert," I said, sobbing.

I hadn't wanted to hurt him and was unsure about what the fuck was even happening, but I had to do it. I had to try to be on my own and find myself. I needed to give myself the opportunity to choose what I needed when I needed it.

Suzanne offered me the spare downstairs bedroom and bath in the house she shared with her partner, Kevin. She convinced me that it was tucked away from the rest of the house, private, and not an inconvenience to them.

So I moved in, vowing to use the time to figure out the next steps, whatever those might be.

Jay was my bright light. Not only had I imposed my life on him, I had reconstructed it so that we could be together, though there was no need to address those moves. I had started production on the film *Caffeine*, an intense indie film about a group of people in a coffee shop in London. Working with a voice coach, I learned to speak with a Northern English accent and stepped into a role that required me to push all of the severe emotions I was dealing with at that moment way into the background so I could be someone else. It was a seriously fucked-up way of coping.

Days and nights were a surreal blend of the new. I lived at Suzanne's but saw Jay and stayed with him as much as I could. All of a sudden I was crazy about this guy who until recently had been my hot Pilates teacher. Jay was a fairly shy individual. He didn't like all the flashiness that seemed to come with me: the paparazzi, the invitations to openings and events, the work schedule, the long conversations with my agent, discussions of fittings, hair, makeup, and photo shoots. One day I gave him several expensive shirts I had bought at the Melrose boutique Fred Segal. He didn't want them or my money or my fame.

To his credit, it made him uncomfortable. He was a guy who was working to put himself through school. I had no idea what sacrifices he had made. I may not have realized it, but this was about me. I couldn't just date him. I wanted him. And to keep him I used the thing that had always gotten me my way—sex. I was too damaged at the time to understand that I had seized him as a replacement for a marriage I never fit into instead of going off on my own and working on myself, which was the reason I had given Robert for leaving.

I saw Jay as a kind of guru. I adopted his regimen of acupuncture and Chinese herbs, believing they would provide the path to the wellness I sought. I pictured my entire being transformed into a perfect state. With me, it was always about perfection. Every single choice I made was based on the idea that I could get there—and quickly.

When I received an offer to film a regional commercial in Sydney, Australia, I jumped at the chance to travel there and invited Jay to join me.

He was from Perth, and I thought he might like the opportunity to see his friends and family in Sydney. Selfishly, I imagined the two of us enjoying a romantic vacation together and returning to the States as a couple, which was what I wanted so desperately. I was looking for my own place when Jay called and said he was in. This was perfect. I thought back to when Robert showed me around his childhood home in Braunschweig. Now Jay would show me around Sydney, introduce me to his family and friends, and we would become a couple.

The production flew us to Australia in first class and put us up in a hotel near the Sydney Opera House. Some sixteen hours after leaving Los Angeles, we arrived at our hotel, where we were shown to a suite with a living room, a bedroom, and the most wondrous view of the harbor. I was mad about this man, totally lost in lust with him, and I had him all to myself in this fabulous room thousands of miles from home. We fell back on the bed, exhausted in the best possible way. It was all too perfect.

And that's when I decided I had to share a secret that I had kept from Jay up to this point. It required summoning all the strength and courage I had in me, but I didn't have a choice. I let him know that I had herpes. I wanted him to know how and why. It was important to me because I'd never had a choice about getting it. I trusted Tyler, who never admitted his bullshit ways. The fact he couldn't keep his dick in his pants became my lifelong problem. Every time I got too stressed or anxious, I broke out in my rear and was reminded in the most painful way of the abuse and indeed the hideous disease he had inflicted on me.

So I had to tell Jay. I assured him that he was safe and that I was responsible about it all. I explained that I would never wish a moment of what I went through upon anyone else, even my worst enemy. It was all so unfair, but that's what it was. I was stuck with this stain, this symbol of degradation, and though I never would have been able to tell him the details about what I went through with Tyler, I had a responsibility to be honest about this thing.

Jay was quiet. He was still next to me on the bed, motionless, while taking in the information. But I felt his energy shift. He switched to a sitting position, still without saying anything but clearly thinking, and then he stood up and walked away from the bed—and away from me. I could see he was feeling defensive and disengaging from me and this suddenly awkward situation. I didn't know if he saw me as the enemy or something else, and I wouldn't have blamed him for thinking of me in that way or one altogether different.

Given what he was expecting and what I had just sprung on him after hours of travel, he had a right. But this was my greatest fear—rejection. And by him.

Inside my head, I went into defensive mode. I wasn't going to beg anyone to be with me, including Jay. I told myself that I had been through enough and I would rather be alone than with someone who thought I was gross, damaged goods. But the truth was I didn't know how to be alone and I felt like I was about to lose my mind. I couldn't believe this was happening all the way on the other side of the world. I had arranged this whole trip, including flights and accommodations for travel up the coast to the Daintree Rainforest, the oldest in the world. And now I saw the picture shattering into a million pieces.

Eventually I got off the bed and walked into the living room, where Jay was sitting on the sofa. He looked tense and confused and conflicted, as I'd expected. I felt the same way, except I was also angry and switching into victimhood. Didn't he even consider what it was like for me to have to deal with this? Did he think I wanted to have to deal with this?

My anger built until I exploded.

"You know what? If you're so fucking unhappy, then just go! If you don't want to be here, then just go! Get the fuck out of here!"

I was damaged in so many more ways than I was willing or able to admit, and I gave him no choice. I opened the hotel room door and threw his bags into the hallway. He still hadn't said a word. But he got up from the sofa and slowly walked toward the door.

I don't think he wanted to leave, but the situation had escalated to the point where there weren't any alternatives, not at that moment, and he shuffled out the door, turning back and facing me like a sad child before I slammed it shut. It was nighttime when I dragged myself back into the bedroom and fell back down on the bed. I knew this had been a horrendous start to a trip that was intended to be a dream. I shut my eyes, hoping that I would wake up in the morning and find out this had been one big, disgusting nightmare.

DOWN UNDER

When I woke, I was still in the same bed, in that same hotel room, all the way across the world. I lay there and was an absolute mess. The tears finally came pouring out. Exhausted by the shock and stress of the night before, I had slipped quickly into a sound sleep. But now that it was daylight, I needed to figure out what I was going to do. I obsessed about all the arrangements I had made, but they masked the real issue. I didn't want to be alone.

The whole episode with Jay could have been an opportunity. It was a clear message that I needed to be honest with myself, not some guy; and that I needed to be able to spend time with myself and not need a relationship to prop me up. I told myself that he couldn't handle my attempt at honesty. Did he think in a million years I would want to be living with that kind of a scar? It was the same shit as always, I told myself.

Except it wasn't. Robert had held me when I broke down sobbing. He supported me going to therapy even if I wasn't truly addressing my issues. I had hoped that Jay would react the same way—and who knows? Maybe he would have if I hadn't insisted he leave. It was all so damn emotional and volatile and fucking embarrassing. I didn't know what to do next, and so I did what I always did when that happened. I called Chuck.

Despite the huge time difference, I reached him. I practically melted from gratitude upon hearing his voice. He talked me down and helped me focus on the trip and handling all the details. I needed his practicality to override my emotional state. Secure that I had a plan to move forward, I veered back to Jay. I still wanted to speak to him, try to make amends, and maybe, just maybe, get back on track with him. The crazy thing was that I still cared for him with what felt like love.

After saying goodbye to Chuck, I contemplated the next call, to Jay. He answered his phone and my heart sank at the sound of his voice. He was at his sister's in Sydney, he said. I took that as a good sign. However, I instantly felt embarrassed. Did his sister know about me? Did she know *about* me? What was I to say or do? I wanted to come to some understanding and resolution about what had happened, I said, and perhaps, maybe, hopefully, resume our trip. He invited me over to his sister's so we could speak in person.

Within an hour, the two of us were talking in a little sunroom at his sister's house. I apologized for my behavior as soon as I got there. Once we were alone, I let him know how much I cared for him. He took my hand and said he understood the deep hurt I had suffered and the bravery it took to open up to him. In turn, he suggested we continue the trip together as friends. I was hesitant, though I hoped he couldn't tell. I clearly didn't want to be his friend, but I also wanted to go on this trip. I knew it would be magical. And I hoped that it would cast a spell that would bring us back together.

Me as a newborn with
my godmother, whom
I'm named after.

Me, around one year old, playing with the daffodils that grew all
around our home Hilltop in Newport, Rhode Island.

Me, having fun doing garden chores with my great-aunt Maria on the grounds of Hilltop.

Sitting inside Hilltop for
a little photo shoot.

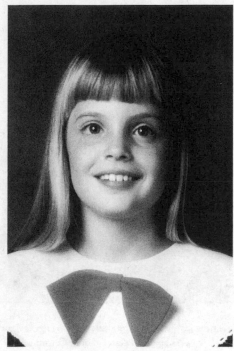

Me, around fourth grade, for my school photo in Rhode Island.

Me, around twelve years old, swinging on the thick vines on our property near where we would build our home in Charleston, South Carolina, before the innocence was lost.

Getting involved with the local modeling agency and taking part in a parade in Charleston, South Carolina.

Winning at the modeling competition in Hiltonhead.

Me, around fourteen years old, when the toughness had begun to take hold.

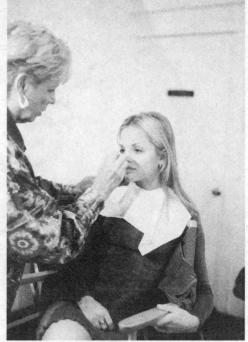

Me, in Los Angeles, getting my makeup done after booking a role on *Boy Meets World*.

The cover page to the original book, *The Great Peace*.

Me, in high school, when the drugs were having a clear effect.

My fifteen-year-old self creating an ode to her guru in another journal I had.

Me, around sixteen years old, driving to a rave with Gabbs.

Rave Daze.

Always out on the prowl with Gabbs. Curlicues tacked down to the sides of my face.

After meeting Stephanie and bringing Gabbs along to be in her clothing line lookbook. I rolled my ankle a dozen times in these wild platforms I owned.

The final result for Stephanie's store, Evolve, on Melrose Avenue. Space aliens!

Me, around the time I was married to and living with Robert, with Stephanie for Halloween.

TRUST

What happened was all the magic I could have asked for. After landing up north, Jay seemed to come back to me. He came across as lighter, present, and happy to be with me. I matched his attitude and very shortly things progressed right back to where we were before heading to Australia. Not only did he become my lover again, he was the most incredible man I had been with. He was everything to me and made my life feel exactly the way I had dreamed. I was out of the dead end, past the darkness, and happy.

We took a ferry to an island where I had found a small B and B. We met the owners, a sweet old French couple who had come to Cairnes years before to make the Daintree their home and livelihood. I complimented them on finding their slice of heaven. When they asked if we were newlyweds, we quickly explained we were friends, make that good friends, but I allowed myself a moment of fantasizing trading wedding bands with Jay.

Our trip also included a visit to an exotic fruit farm, where they grew the weirdest fruits I'd ever heard of, including one that tasted exactly like chocolate. In the store where they sold homemade ice cream, Jay and I spent what felt like half the day tasting and selecting just the right flavor combination. Then it was off to the Great Barrier Reef, an experience that was like touring an underwater museum of rare and unbelievably beautiful artworks. It also caused me to face one of my greatest fears, which only deepened the bond I felt toward Jay.

When I was younger and living in Charleston, I went through a period when I had horrible recurring nightmares. In the one I had most frequently, I would be trapped inside an old house high on a hill with a bright red door. I made my way down the stairs toward the front door, where there was a dresser covered with all types of telephones. I started picking up each and every phone, shouting out my street address, yet I was never able to get a dial tone. Every single phone was dead. The front door was locked, and when I turned around to look for another way out, I came face-to-face with an old man and an old woman, who were spewing hate at me. As the woman got closer, she cackled, "You'll never get out of here." And I knew she was right. I would never make it out of that house. I was trapped forever.

The other recurring nightmare I had started soon after I suffered what felt like near-fatal pain after being stung by a Portuguese man o' war in the ocean. I was twelve years old and with my family on Kiawah Island outside Charleston. We were spending the day at the beach. I was nervous about swimming in these waters, but encouraged by a mother and daughter in the nearby shallows, I went diving for sand dollars. Suddenly I felt the most excruciating pain ever. I screamed and cried out for help, but none came. The mother and daughter looked at me and laughed, thinking I was just being silly and dramatic. But I wasn't, and as the pain worsened, I managed to swim to catch a wave and make it onto the shore, where I crashed onto the sand and yelled for my family.

A lifeguard arrived first and threw the contents of a big bucket over me. I couldn't move; I was paralyzed. Then my brothers came into view. They stood over me, tauntingly chanting, "You're gonna die! You're gonna die!" I was dumbstruck. How can you laugh at someone who needs assistance? How can you see a young girl who has fallen off her bicycle because her foot slipped and caught inside the spokes, flinging her into the middle of a road with traffic, and drive on by without stopping, as had happened to me earlier that same year?

It was all fodder for the nightmare that started after the jellyfish incident. In it, I would find myself all alone in an ocean of red blood. I clung to a small piece of wood, with my legs dangling below, and told myself to kick. I filled with fear and panic that some creature beneath the surface was about to bite into my legs and rip them off. Though I eventually ceased having the dream, it left me deathly afraid of the ocean and even the deep end of swimming pools.

That fear followed me out to the Great Barrier Reef with Jay. I told him that I wanted no part in scuba diving no matter how magnificent the water and once-in-a-lifetime this visit might be. I could handle beaches, tide pools, and even snorkeling in shallow water. But not here in the middle of the ocean. He was patient with me during the hour-long boat ride out there. That part was glorious. The water, the breeze, the sunshine. It was just magical. And Jay was next to me, warm and toasty in the sun, as we listened to the Police's song "Walking on the Moon" play over the speaker system.

Every so often I caught myself thinking about what had happened our first night in Sydney, but I pushed it away and wanted to feel like it had never happened. The test came when our guide announced that we could go down about twenty-five feet with scuba equipment or snorkel along the surface. Jay wanted to scuba dive. I saw he was supremely confident in his physical ability, and he encouraged me to feel the same.

I put on a brave face and then I put on the scuba gear. The guide showed us how to fall back into the ocean and then helped the two of us get into position on the back of the boat. I started talking to myself: Take a deep breath, let your body relax, and trust. Trust that you're going to fall back into the water and be okay. Just do it. Just lean back and let gravity pull you. Though terrified, I finally took a big gulp of air and fell backward into the water.

The weight of all the gear I had on instantly pulled me deep beneath the surface. At first, I panicked. I felt vulnerable and out of my comfort zone. All I saw was water—all around me, above and below—and I felt like I was drowning. That's when the trust kicked in. I heard the instructions I had been given back on the boat, and I followed each of the steps. I worked to regulate my breathing. Slow and easy. Trust the equipment. Then swim. Feel the control you do have. Trust your diving buddy. I gave a thumbs-up to Jay.

I did all of this and suddenly it got easier, even comfortable. I was apprehensive and on alert, but I wasn't as scared. I moved around, felt the current, floated along, and found myself marveling at this amazing undersea environment and, not incidentally, at myself for having pushed past my fears in order to have this experience. If only I was able to be as brave on the surface, where I was supposedly more comfortable and secure but let my fears and past horrors control me rather than trusting myself to explore what would happen if I pushed past them.

Later, I snorkeled along the surface, figuring one massive challenge for the day was enough. As we returned to land, I curled up next to Jay. I felt so grateful for the way he had helped me conquer the demons that made me fearful of swimming in the ocean. I told myself that I had never been happier or more at peace—and maybe that was true.

Something else was also true, something I chose to ignore, and that was the way I gave all the credit to Jay and none to myself.

Why was my perception so warped?

I guess I knew why, but I clearly wasn't able to dive into those waters.

LOOKING

Saying goodbye to our Australian vacation was hard. Despite the rocky start, it had turned out to be everything I had hoped. Jay and I had become a couple and I felt like we had a real chance at carving out a future together back home. But Jay had a different reaction. As soon as we got to the airport to check in, he changed. My upbeat, holistic healer-slash-hero seemed depressed, deflated, and massively confused.

I had seen him pass in and out of moods, but nothing like this. I couldn't understand why he was miserable after such a wonderful trip and how everything turned so completely and suddenly. It became clearer when he spoke of how hard things were, the world being the way it was, with people like him having to work hard, and despite all that, it still was a struggle.

I understood he was reacting to the way everything on this luxurious trip had been handed to us. It was similar to the reaction he'd had when I bought him the shirts at Fred Segal. He wasn't altogether wrong, but this was my life and, as I tried to explain, perks like those we had enjoyed were balanced by uncertainty, insecurity, and countless reasons the work could suddenly dry up. But I hadn't experienced a dynamic like this before, one where I had to be the strong one.

I had a sixteen-hour flight to try to figure it out. My effort went on like a self-help tape without end. I let him know that everything was going to be okay, that it was normal to wish life were an eternal vacation, and so on. I threw every cliché in the book at him, hoping something would stick and we could go back to being the same Jay and Mena of the past week. But that was wishful thinking. Not long after we arrived back in LA, a different vision of us emerged, and it wasn't the version I wanted.

HEAVY-DUTY DETOX

Of all the memorable things that happened in Australia, the one I thought about most after getting back to LA was when Jay and I had been asked if we were newlyweds. I reveled in the fantasy.

I should have known better. It was time for me to find a new home. I told Sigal how happy I always felt by the beach. I described Australia and said it reminded me of being in St. John when I was little and carefree. The energy by the beach was healing and I wanted its presence to help me with the next chapter of my life if possible. With Sigal's help, I found a home in Venice. Before I signed the papers, though, I had to speak with Robert and find out if he was going to be asking me for spousal support in our divorce.

Because I had been the main source of income in our marriage, he was entitled to ask for support, meaning I would pay him a set amount every month for half of the time we had been married. In our case, that was two and a half years. My accountant advised me to ask, and I called him from the guest bedroom in Suzanne and Kevin's home. I was uncomfortable making the call, but I believed he would still want to be on friendly terms with me, wanting the best for me as I did for him, and so I was taken aback when he said, "Give me one good reason why I shouldn't get everything I'm entitled to."

I felt like I had been hit and started to panic. I had found this house in Venice; to me, it was an opportunity to begin my own life and write my own story. I didn't see the way I was simply swapping out my life. I traded

153

Robert for Jay. I wanted this house in Venice because it resembled the house where I'd lived with Robert. I was sick and tired of giving everything to everyone else, which was the way I saw my life, and that included Robert. I'd left without asking for anything, the majority of which I'd paid for. But I didn't care about possessions, I was trying to find my own happiness. Why did he want to take every penny from me that he "deserved"? Hadn't I given enough?

While we sorted things out, I got sick. After getting together with Jay, I'd started taking the Chinese herbs his doctor prescribed and doing acupuncture. The acupuncture treatments had been amazing. During one visit, the doctor put a needle into my lower back and I broke down. It was as if he had opened a spigot and emotions poured out. I was embarrassed at the way I sobbed, heaving on the table, but apparently I needed to let all that go. Jay agreed, and I believed I was speeding toward enlightenment and greater health and potential.

Except, unwittingly, the herbs I took made me feel like I had a bladder infection. My gynecologist ran several tests that all came back negative. I worried when the symptoms persisted for several more weeks and turned into a real pain. Jay explained that in Chinese medicine, the organs correspond to different emotions, and the bladder, he said, represents fear.

Which made sense. I was going through this divorce from Robert and it was manifesting in my body. Given my devotion to the practice at the time, I accepted this diagnosis and expected to feel better after Robert and I reached a settlement. In exchange for a lump sum of money, I got my clothes and personal belongings and two woodcuts that I had bought several years back at an art show in New York. I didn't ask for anything else.

It still wasn't that easy. After a few trips to pick up my belongings, Robert changed the locks on me. Dreading the game playing, I corralled Sigal and rented a U-Haul truck so I could get everything in one trip. It was ironic. When I'd moved into my new three-bedroom home in Venice, I had only a futon bed and a candle. It was exciting but the house was empty. After Sigal and I loaded up the U-Haul and unloaded all the stuff in my new place, it still felt empty. Clothes and vases and picture frames do not furnish a house.

I didn't care. These things had sentimental value to me and I was glad to have them back.

Before leaving, I'd been able to straighten out one other issue with Robert. While I had been in Australia, my new publicists had been faxing me every article and picture showing me and Jay on vacation. Because they didn't know I was separated, they were sending them to Robert's house. It came across to him as the ultimate fuck you. Until Robert told me, I'd had no idea. I didn't blame him for being upset, and immediately issued my own cease and desist order.

All that was left to solve was the pain in my bladder. It wasn't going away. I noticed I was down to the last of the herbs I had been taking. It took a few days to refill, which wasn't a big deal, but after I ran out, I noticed the pain went away. I started to feel better. I didn't put two and two together, though. I had been going out of my mind dealing with Robert, moving into my new house, and trying to make it work with Jay. I'd assumed the stress from each had been responsible for the pain. When the pain went away, I figured it was because I was healing and finally moving into this miraculous state of health and awareness.

Jay brought my refill over to the house late one afternoon and I took the usual dose before bed so I'd be back on track to wellness. But when I got up the next morning and went into the bathroom to pee, the pain was back again and worse than ever. There was also a smell this time. I knew things were not right. A light bulb went off. It had to be the herbs. They were the only thing I had taken for months. When I'd run out, I felt better.

I grabbed that bottle and made an emergency appointment with my old nutritionist. I had seen her for years with Robert, but I left her behind when I split with him. After welcoming me back and hearing my story, she looked at the bottle of herbs and sent it out to someone who could translate the ingredients for her. They were all listed in Chinese. The information that came back was worrisome. I had been taking double the amount of herbs she would have normally prescribed, plus there were a bunch of heavy-duty detoxifiers mixed in. The smell in my urine was ammonia. Basically, I had been taking a powerful cocktail that threw off the pH balance in my body.

Jay did not react well when I told him the herbs were making me sick. I think it might have been the beginning of the end for us. He had always had reservations about taking on someone like me—a newly separated, soon-to-be-divorcée client-turned-lover—and now I was questioning his expertise as a healer. To his credit, he said that seeing me get sick had made him question what he was doing with his life. At the same time, it was sort of like I was asking him to choose between me and everything he had been studying.

One night I was on the phone with Sigal. I was recapping Australia, the drama with Robert, my health issues, and how I felt like it was such a mind fuck with Jay. Upset, I said that I didn't know if I had the strength to hold it together.

"Mena, you have to understand the difference between fantasy and reality," she said.

I fell silent. She was right, and it hit me with the force of a giant wave. I had always appreciated the way Sigal could and did call me out on my shit. I had been so enraptured by the thought of Jay and me together and what that life with him would look and even feel like that I had ignored every single sign that we weren't right for each other.

I knew what she meant and took a deep breath.

"Are you okay?" Sigal asked.

"I hope so," I said.

"BY THE WAY . . ."

thought I had it all figured out. To avoid rejection and disappointment, I told myself that I didn't want to be tied to anyone. Instead I would live my life like every single guy out there. As long as I was responsible and safe, and most importantly, honest, I could date and be with whomever I wanted. I was tired of playing nice. Why not be just the same way toward these guys that they had always been to me?

Jay and I were having lunch at a restaurant when I broke the news to him. I wanted an open relationship. Once again, I was trying to have my cake and eat it, too. *I'll get my own place, but we'll stay married.* I was pretending that I didn't care and wanted to be like the guys. But I didn't want to lose Jay either. My feelings for him were still strong. I managed to convince myself this new arrangement was the best way to deal with those conflicted feelings, and I actually thought Jay might go for it, too. What guy didn't want options like those I was offering?

Jay, for one. Surprised, he rejected the arguments I put forth and said if he couldn't be with me exclusively, he could only be my friend. His response was, I suppose, a profession of the love and fidelity that I had pushed for with him. But I was so entrenched in getting what I thought I wanted now that it sailed past me. I was more than a little surprised that a woman could turn the tables and be met with such confusion and disgust. Reluctantly, though, I agreed. We would be friends. *Just friends*, I said.

As my friend, I invited Jay to be my guest at the premiere for my next movie, the Tony Scott–directed film *Domino*. The event was at the Chinese

157

Theatre, off of Hollywood Boulevard, and it was one of those epic, red-carpet nights that studios pour promotion money into. I was provided a row of seats for family and friends. After speaking with the press and posing for pictures, I was ushered to my seat right before the movie started. As I made my way to the middle of the aisle, where I had about a dozen girlfriends, I spotted Jay a few seats away, looking at me like a sad puppy.

He had wanted to sit next to me but the seats were all taken, he said. To avoid a scene, my friends agreed to swap with him and everyone moved so Jay could sit with me. I was thrown off because we were now just friends and, as such, he should have been fine where he was. Then, during the film, we held hands, which confused me further. Had he thought about us not being exclusive and decided he was okay with it?

I didn't get a chance to find out. As soon as the film ended, Jay got up with everyone else and headed toward the lobby. I was with Sigal, making my way through the crowded theater toward him. He was waiting next to the theater entrance. When I got close, I invited him to walk over to the after-party with us. He shook his head and said, "I'm gonna go." Carefully concealing the way I really felt, I said okay. But I was crushed. I held on to Sigal and continued on with my night, faking a smile while crying inside.

Sigal encouraged me to let him go. Sitting at a table surrounded by party-goers, it sounded like the smartest option, if not the only sane one. Then I got a text from Jay. "By the way, you look beautiful tonight. I love you." His sweet note was the nail in the coffin. I read it as the epitome of passive-aggressiveness, and as I told Sigal, I was allergic to such behavior. I grew up with so much of it in my family and it never made me feel safe. I texted him back. "You know what Jay? The people that truly love me are here tonight, with me, to support me, and be with me. You made it all about you tonight." I was better off on my own.

I figured I would find my way like I always did.

CAUGHT IN THE MIDDLE

The next day, I was at home in Venice, sitting in the guesthouse. I had been spending time with my rescue kitties, Sid and Nancy. They had been my steadiest companions for the past few years. I had scooped them up after seeing someone dump them into the street from a car in the hills of Los Feliz and Robert and I had taken them in. Brother and sister tabbies, they were beautiful, sweet, and independent creatures whose daily agenda still included plenty of time for cuddling and affection.

We were kindred souls—and survivors. Shortly after Sigal and I had left Robert's with the U-Haul full of my most precious belongings, Robert showed up at my new house and deposited a bunch of garbage bags across my front lawn. He was about to leave when I spotted him and stepped outside. Quickly, he threw the rest of what he had stuffed in his car on the lawn and drove off. The bags were filled with papers, random beauty and body care items, even single tampons. All stuff that could have been thrown in the garbage, which was what I assumed he thought he was doing in a more figurative manner. But included in the detritus were Sid and Nancy, both of them locked in their carriers. Nancy's included medication for a recent illness.

I brought them inside and then fell onto my knees in the entryway, sobbing until there was a small puddle of tears on the floor. At that time, I had nothing in my house, the floor was cracking beneath me and Jay, and I wanted to scream every time I peed. Why was my life such a fucking mess when all I wanted was calm and order?

After the premiere, though my bladder pain was gone, my life was still every bit as painful and lonely as ever, and I turned to an old friend for relief. I got high. I had been five years sober when I got a hold of some pot and smoked it right up. I had put so much energy into creating the perfect replica of what I imagined my life should be, and here was what it amounted to: me sitting alone in my upstairs bathroom, firing up my bong.

I made one last effort to connect with Jay. One night I called him up and said I wanted him to come over. I was convinced I could handle this laissez-faire approach to relationships and that I was within my rights to order up Jay for sex the way others had done with me. I waited for Jay by the staircase wearing seductive lingerie. He was as appreciative as I had hoped and then some. After admiring me, he said that he loved me.

I didn't want to hear that. Those words were not in the script I had in my head, and when I didn't respond, he pressed the issue by answering for me. "You love me." This was not about love or anything else other than sex, I told myself. I felt righteous and entitled. *Why couldn't we just fuck if that's what it's really all about anyway?* I wondered. Because it wasn't about that for Jay, and though I was loath to admit it, the same was true for me. Finally, after he brought up the L-word again, I flat out said, "No, I don't. I don't love you."

Jay was quiet. Neither of us had anything more to say. Many years passed before I saw him again. I was at an Italian restaurant in Hollywood when I spotted Jay at a table across the dining room with a young woman. I never knew if he also saw me. It was one of those classic bittersweet moments and left me wondering if he remembered only the hurt we inflicted on each other, or if our trip up in the Daintree outshone all the misery and was something he cherished as an amazing life experience, like I did.

Changes of the Chameleon

Constant chattering
These words formed into conversation
What am I saying?
Why am I saying this strife?
All jumbled into an enormous conversation
They never cease.
Cackles from near and deafness would seem beautiful.
Turn around.
Amuse your neighbor.
I copy you, you copy me.
I trust you, you use me.
When we look over our shoulders to create the beauty we lost
    long ago
We cheat.
We cheat in this class of life.
Life 101, then failed.
No continuation.
Only objects.
Only replaced objects.
Only for people. Different colors of brilliance.
I give to you, but the coldness of your chair burns your soul.
Different in every surrounding
Changing with the months and every season.
Chameleon life.
Changes unknown, unstoppable.

Remnants of truth left inside.

Yet each truth inside represents a different color than the one
   present outside.

Changes of the chameleon.

3/6/96

TEMESCAL

let myself drift. I made a promise to myself to not get into another committed relationship, and I kept it. I went out with my girlfriends. I wanted to heal from *everything*.

I bought a bong and smoked regularly again. It was the only thing that made the pain go away. I gave myself homeopathic pain medication shots. I hiked Temescal Canyon, a mile-plus loop in the Pacific Palisades that let me slip into the folds of mountains and disappear into the wilderness. The trail passed by a secret waterfall that fell with ever-changing force depending on the rainfall and water level and produced the most beautiful sounds, a rhythmic music that was never the same score twice but always and instantly relaxing.

It was nature beckoning with its gentle touch. Come close. Sit down. Breathe. Connect and heal.

I took to laying a drop cloth by the river and painting. I was trying to make sense of my life. This little patch of canyon became my View-Master, allowing me to see the beauty that I longed to see and feel in my own life. I was still seeing a therapist but she didn't seem as helpful as time in the wild. I let myself go only so far in sessions with her. Out in the canyon, I let go of everything and lost myself in the quiet, soaring through treetops in the rush of wind, following birds until they disappeared, or listening to the sound of water flowing downriver and letting my soul drift to hitch a ride.

Sometimes Sigal and Limor joined me for a hike, but mostly I ventured off on my own, eager to get out of my large home and away from the phone and melt into the holy power of this outdoor cathedral. On one hike, I found a small bench tucked away off the trail path. How had I never seen it before? It was pretty secluded, situated amongst a lot of foliage. I sat down with the fresh air caressing my face and I cried. I hadn't planned on bawling like that and didn't know I needed to, but I let it come out of me, my own waterfall of frustration.

When Sigal, Limor, and I had hiked the canyon, they gushed about how much they cherished the time they had alone with themselves. I envied their self-confidence and comfort with who they were. Not that they weren't working on themselves, but they liked who they were. I couldn't begin to imagine what that felt like, but I wanted it for myself. Given the amount of time I spent on my own, I didn't understand why I couldn't find that sort of acceptance. Forget contentment. Never mind peace. Those were the ultimate goals, but I looked at the inner calm and love I desired with a sense of evanescence. It was there. Or was it?

One day Sigal and Limor invited me to a dance and music event at the Queen Mary in Long Beach. I accepted. It would be my first night out since my final confrontation with Jay a little more than three months earlier. I had been treating my bladder pain with homeopathy, with marijuana, and it felt manageable. I was divorced, over Jay, starting to feel better physically, and, as I told my girlfriends when I said I would go with them to the dance, life was starting to feel worth living again.

I wanted to dance.

The whole night was spectacular. The best part was that I met a guy named Mike. I hadn't planned on connecting with anyone and was generally in the mindset that I needed to live life on my own before riding tandem again. But it happened. He was a dancer, one of a relatively small number of amazing pros who competed that night in a breakdancing battle. He was extremely handsome, and fit, and wore his hair in dreadlocks. I walked right up to him, said hi, and we talked late into the night.

Because it was my first time out in a minute and the environment was pretty crazy, the ladies and I decided to leave early. So we missed seeing the big announcement that Mike and his dance crew had won their competition.

But I had given Mike my number and he texted me the good news. Once I was home, we connected again and talked more.

My mind was completely blown when I asked him what sign he was. I had been surrounded by Scorpios—Robert, Jay—and when Mike told me his birthday, I reacted by throwing the phone against the wall. It was the same day as Jay's. Incredible! Too freaky. How could I fall right in with another Scorpio?

I walked across the room and picked the phone back up. Mike was still on the line. It typified our relationship. He was always there for me. Eventually I had to literally push him away. We spent years together. A sweet and gentle guy, he lived in Las Vegas. I spent countless hours driving through the desert to spend time with him. He shared a house with a friend of his and his friend's girlfriend, but it had enough space for us to have our privacy.

Every day, he and his friends met up and practiced. For them, dance was a mix of art and discipline. It showed. Their performances were spellbinding articulations of passion, joy, spirit, and feeling through movement. Their crew won almost every competition they entered. I was enamored of his ability and proud of him. He had unique qualities and an infectious spirit that he shared in exuberant bursts of movement, and I found out where he got all that when he introduced me to his family.

Mike was Hispanic, and his family lived in El Paso, a beautiful city on the Rio Grande in the western part of Texas. I went there several times, including one Christmas holiday. Each time, his immediate and extended family welcomed me with hugs and a warmth that was wonderful to experience. They afforded me the privilege of seeing the way a healthy, loving family worked. Their home crackled with laughter and conversation; meals were central to the day's activities, especially dinner. Everyone gathered, ate, talked, asked one another questions, ventured opinions.

I envied the love and support Mike's parents gave him. They took pride in their son's talent, drive, and accomplishments. No wonder he moved with such uninhibited exuberance, I thought. In contrast, I saw the way I lived: an empty home, getting high by myself, trying to escape the problems stemming from not having that kind of nurturing, stable, loving foundation.

Did people know how to love that way instinctively? Or was it learned? Could it be relearned? I wish I could say I knew. What I did come to learn, though, was that when I eventually cheated on Mike, his heart broke and so did mine.

MIKE

was never one to cheat. There was that time when I was on location, away from Tyler, and I slept with an extra. But I didn't count that as cheating because we had called Tyler in flagrante so he could be a part of it. But Tyler hadn't known about my costar, who, as I looked back, had been an attempt to break out of the sick cycle I was in, though ultimately I wasn't strong enough and I stayed in the relationship with Tyler until I bounced into others.

Being with Mike, though, was sweet and easy and loving. He didn't smoke pot, but he never minded that I did. He was so easygoing that I got frustrated by always getting my way. It was also difficult negotiating what was essentially a long-distance relationship. Mike frequently drove to LA from his Las Vegas home and almost as often I made the long three-hour drive on I-15 to see him. As straight as those lines were through the desert, I wasn't sure where the relationship would go.

I definitely wasn't thinking about getting married. I wasn't sure if I ever would again. I tried not to think too far ahead and get overwhelmed.

When I had to travel, I tried to bring Mike. I got him a place to dance in the Heatherette Spring 2007 fashion show, which I walked in during New York's Fashion Week. He was amazing and it was pretty epic to work together. But then I went on location to make a movie and slept with one of my costars and the spell was broken. I told myself that I was living in the moment, not cheating. I was free, empowered, living life as it presented itself. No one controlled me.

Wasn't this how the system worked?

The movie was shooting in another country. I went there by myself, prepared to stay for several months. My goodbye to Mike was sweet and heartfelt but layered with unspoken ambiguity of no commitment. I got on the plane excited to be so far away from home and able to immerse myself in a new culture completely on my own. In what is one of the most intoxicating perks of the movie business, I arrived feeling liberated from the past, from my life, from the expectations and anxieties of life in LA.

This was real freedom. To be a floater in the world. For the next few months, I could forget about what everyone else was doing and quit trying to desperately emulate what I thought was appropriate and just live.

I quickly sparked to my costar. Attractive, smart, witty, he was unlike anyone that I had ever been with. During our filming schedule, production stopped for a local holiday and gave us the opportunity to spend time at a small luxurious resort outside the city. I signed up, eager to spoil myself at the spa and swim in the pool. My costar made a similar plan. After some fun, flirtatious splashing in the pool, we continued the playtime back in my hotel room.

There, the situation turned into something quite unexpected and impossible to ignore. It was simply the hottest, most amazing sex I'd ever had. Life changing? I don't know. Unforgettable? Absolutely. I remember turning over in bed and breathlessly thinking, *Wow*. I was immensely satisfied with myself for living without restrictions or rules and feeling like I did.

And then I burst into tears.

As soon as it was over, I started to cry and couldn't stop.

I was embarrassed to be suddenly so uncontrollably emotional in front of this guy who I didn't really know, and I was completely naked and vulnerable. How awkward to put him in that situation. But he didn't care that I had a boyfriend. That was assumed. What he did care about was me. He stayed and caressed my arm and back, comforted me, listened to me whimper an apology, held me in an attempt to share his strength, and told me that everything would be okay. He gave me such a beautiful moment.

We slept together a few more times without anyone finding out, always sneaking to each other's room, where the sex was incredible. We knew we wouldn't have a chance in the outside world. Strangely, that made it easy and safe to care for each other. And want each other. Knowing this wasn't going to last beyond this moment in time.

And it didn't. When filming was over, we returned to our lives in Los Angeles with great memories of good work and a tender friendship.

ON LOCATION

Things became uncomfortable for me with Mike. He deserved better than me. My emotional life was a world of extremes where I limited how much of another person's feelings I let into my own heart. Mike was a prime example of a thoughtful, caring man who I kept at a distance while enjoying the affection he was willing to show me as long as it was convenient for me. I knew it wasn't fair to him, and I didn't want to be cruel.

I was saved by another film that took me back to Europe. I was going to spend several months in this foreign country, living near the sea and working on a role that posed daily challenges mentally and emotionally. The material felt personal. It was interesting how making art often imitated life, and sometimes consumed it. My costar was tall and dark and handsome. He had a bold and infectious presence and a smile that served as an invitation to enter. It wasn't long before the two of us became physical with each other.

I viewed this as my right to independence. I was an adult, living life on my own terms, without any promises or attachments. I felt like it was a game, and that I was winning if I made sure no one ever had control over me. It was a cold, heartless, and empty way to live, and I didn't see that all my actions indicated I craved the opposite. I was in a relationship with my costar for almost the entire time we were on location. We didn't speak of it in those terms. I didn't want to know how he regarded me. Asking would have required me to become vulnerable. It might also have led to something wonderful. I'd never know.

It was easier and safer to assume he was like any other guy and didn't really care for me. It was only about the sex. What else was I good for? Apparently much more than I thought. But then I screwed it up.

One night I found a bar that was playing reggae music, which I was heavily into at the time. I felt like dancing and went in by myself. My costar had his friend visiting him from back home, and I'd figured that his guy time was more important than spending time with me, so I had headed out to the bar on my own. I had a great time that night and hit it off with the DJ, who was beautiful and elegant. We hung out together the rest of the night.

When it was time to go home, I invited him back to my hotel for a one-night stand. I had never met a stranger and brought them back to my room alone. It was odd, new, and the most exciting thing I had ever done. I knew I would never see this man again, but I enjoyed celebrating and exploring our lust and attraction for each other. I also liked learning about him: he was a recent arrival from Mozambique, into music and life; he spoke of his home in Africa, his family, and his hopes and fears about being far away from everything that was familiar to him. At the end of the night, we said goodbye and it was lovely.

The next day my costar knocked on my hotel room door. He was upset that he hadn't heard from me the previous night. He asked if I had gone out. I wasn't sure whether he was angry or concerned, but I stepped back, feeling defensive while trying to play dumb and avoid having to say anything. While contemplating my options, he got straight to the point. Had I been with someone else? I considered lying, but I didn't want to. Besides, I didn't feel like I had done anything wrong. Though I feared his reaction, I looked straight into his eyes and said, "Yes." In that instant, his spirit deflated and I saw everything we had disappear.

He was hurt, but it was the last thing I'd wanted to do to him. It was also the last thing I expected. My sense of self-worth was so low that I didn't think he cared about me. But when I saw that I had hurt him, I reacted the only way that I knew how: I fought it. I didn't want to take responsibility for something I didn't want to acknowledge.

"It's not like I'm your girlfriend or anything," I said.

Another direct hit.

He had no choice but to fire back.

"You're right! You're not!" he exclaimed, before turning and storming down the hall.

After shutting the door, I stood in my hotel room and ran through the usual rationalizations and reasons I shouldn't feel guilty. I was a grown woman, who wasn't married, and I could make my own, responsible decisions regarding who I slept with. Why should I have to ask permission when I had always been the one who was cheated on? Why did I have to feel wrong for not calling him when we weren't in a defined relationship? No matter what I said, though, I couldn't get past the idea that I had needlessly hurt him and ruined something special for myself.

Back in Los Angeles, he went on to find a serious relationship and the happy ending he deserved. I found myself making another desperate attempt at marriage and repeating past mistakes in the process. It felt like I just couldn't ever get it right.

SIMONE

settled back into home life in Los Angeles and marveled at the beauty of my home in Venice. I was excited to be back in my life. I saw Mike a few times, but I quickly put up a wall between us without explaining why. In one of the scenes at the end of the movie I had just finished, my character shaved her head. I did it in real life. Ironically, the scene didn't make the final cut, but I returned to LA with shorn locks and a bold, empowered attitude from having done it.

The paparazzi had a field day with it when they spotted me and my sharply different look lunching with a friend in Beverly Hills. This was around the same time that Brittany Spears had shaved her head. Although our circumstances were vastly different, I understood what she was trying to accomplish. After my head was shaved and I got past the initial shock and awe, I felt liberated from the way I looked and the way I was supposed to look. It was empowering.

I loved how strong it made me feel. The long blonde hair that I had prized my whole life and that others had always complimented was gone. In its place was me, just me, all of me, the real me, the what-you-see-is-what-you-get me, no hiding, pretending, putting it up or down, and I loved it.

I took this new look to Toronto, where I was hosting an event. After checking in to my hotel, I wanted to get some pot. I called a friend of mine who knew someone who knew someone and so on, until I was connected to a guy who I was told would come through. I figured why not be gracious and invite him to the event? It was going to be a fun night in Yorkville. He could bring a friend. I'd put them on the list.

His name was Simone, and I thought he was cute. He was of medium height, with dark, tan skin, blond hair, and light eyes. He lived in Toronto with his parents and two brothers, but they were close to extended family in Italy, he said. Having recently been in Europe, I was intrigued, and Simone, who crackled with energy and humor and a funky little laugh, promised to tell me more later.

I didn't care or think twice about the fact behind our meeting, that he was dealing me pot; we had an amazing night and we spent every day together after that, until I had to head back home. We hung out in my hotel room, got stoned, and one thing obviously led to another. He was a great lover, and I was hooked. I wanted him in my life and he seemed to fit.

Simone felt the same way. Soon after we met, he wanted to take me to Italy, to show me his country, and to meet the rest of his family. Hearing that made me think of the way traveling in Europe had been with Robert, and I immediately grew nostalgic for being with someone able to share their easy familiarity with a foreign country. I conveniently failed to remember the way I had paid for all of my travels with Robert and continued to pay after we were no longer together.

My understanding of my finances was no better than it had been in the past. I never asked questions. I never learned what I had and what I spent. I never considered the well might run low or even dry up. Ever since I made *American Pie* and wrote out a check for thirty thousand dollars to purchase my first car, the Toyota 4Runner, I simply indulged in whatever I wanted at the moment. With Robert, I spent tens of thousands of dollars fixing up the guesthouse, landscaping the front and back yards, and buying new high-end furniture. When I left, I didn't take any of it. I thought nothing of walking into Chloé or Yves Saint Laurent and dropping five thousand dollars. Shoes for thirteen hundred dollars? They were beautiful. They were art. I wanted them. So why not?

I ignored the painful reality of having seen my family go from living in a stately Rhode Island mansion to a crummy apartment in Burbank, California, where we shopped at the 99-cent store. I clung to the romance of what my life had been like when I was a little child twirling through our ballroom and picking up shells as I skipped along the shore, believing anything and everything was possible and beautiful. I didn't just chase the high; I chased the fantasy.

When I finally furnished my new home in Venice, I spent without considering the price. Six thousand for a coffee table? So what? It was perfect. A vacation with Jay? No problem. Mike was driving in from Vegas in a crappy car? When I bought a new car for myself, I simply added a second one to the tab and gave it to him. Problem solved. Then, after Simone mentioned going to Italy, I was swept away with desire—for the trip, for the unexpected excitement he introduced to my life, and for him.

"Let's just go," I said.

Of course, the trip was a disaster—the way everything else with him would turn out. I only wish I had stopped to see this and ask why.

ANOTHER ATTEMPT

Simone and I had been in Italy only a few days when guilt got the better of me. I needed to make a difficult phone call. I had to call Mike and tell him it was over between us once and for all. Both of us had been hanging on in our own way and no doubt for our own reasons, but I knew it was wrong and the weight of that hit me while Simone and I were walking around Rome, so much so that I could feel my legs grow heavy and my gait start to slow and plod to the point that I felt I might actually lose my ability to walk and stand if I didn't address this situation. Immediately.

Standing there in the streets of Rome, with people bustling all around me, I was able to erect a wall around me and dial Mike. Given the time difference, I had no idea what he was doing, where he was, or if he would even answer, but he picked up. And when I heard him say hello, I turned into a block of coldhearted steel and without much of a prelude, I told him that I wasn't in love with him anymore.

It was such a horrible moment, trying to show compassion when I didn't feel like I wanted to, all I wanted was for it to be over. Then it ended. I hung up and went back to Simone, taking his hand in mine and feeling like I was in love as we continued walking down the boulevard. I still cringe at the way I was able to deceive myself and the hurt I must have inflicted on Mike. As for me and Simone, our time in Italy was magnificent, beautiful, opulent, delicious, and all on my dime.

Simone introduced me to his family and took me around all of Rome, showing me the best and brightest of it, and we fell deeper into each other. I had met Simone through a friend in the music industry, the same as Simone, and he fancied himself a promoter. He had once hosted a massive club night in Italy but had wanted to expand to more countries and tried from his home in Canada. He was glued to his phone, frenetically texting or talking, always networking, and suddenly I was part of it.

After the trip, Simone and I visited my mother in the south. She had moved there several years before, and I was eager for her to meet my new boyfriend. I was always desperate for a real connection with my mother and I felt like she would be proud of me this time, in finding someone younger and charming like Simone, the way that it hadn't been with how my family perceived Robert. Still embarrassed that I was a divorcée at twenty-five, I felt like I had gotten it right this time. In my mind, Simone was different. He was someone who could live in the same fantastic and oh-so-glamorous way I did. I gushed that Simone had family in Toronto and Rome, making it seem like we would be jetting between those two international cities and my own place in Venice, itself known as an enclave for artists.

One afternoon, while Simone and I were walking through the city's quaint downtown, we darted into a little jewelry store featuring local artisans. I admired a ring made of engraved sterling with a clear quartz stone. It slipped on my finger easily, and I cooed that it was magical and elegant. Later that night, Simone surprised me with the ring. He had gone back to the store and bought it. He called it a promise ring. I put it on and felt more connected to him than ever. I felt like I was, finally, structuring my life correctly.

But two weeks later, the ring was gone. After parting, I'd returned home to Venice and waited for Simone to visit. It didn't take long. I was eager to share my life with him, and I enjoyed having him with me, until I didn't. We never talked about the length of his stay, but it lasted longer than I expected and then everything got on my nerves. One day we were driving back to my place and got in an argument. It quickly boiled into a nasty spat, and as we came to a stop at an intersection, I ripped off his promise ring and threw it out the window.

Shades of my childhood when I was a first grader in Rhode Island and a boy in class who was the butt of jokes greeted me one morning with a ring. In front of all our classmates, he asked me to marry him. Mortified, I ripped the ring from his little fingers, chucked it out the window next to me, and screamed, "No!" Months later, his mother told mine that I had broken his little heart. Even then, I had pushed love away.

Only this time it was Simone who screamed, No! I drove straight home. I was done. The relationship was over. I saw so clearly all the ways we weren't right for each other and I knew I needed to get away from him and have my space. After parking in front of my house, I told him to get out of the car, get his stuff from the house, and leave. But Simone didn't budge. The more I yelled, the calmer he appeared, almost as if he enjoyed seeing me lose control. I went wild with rage. Every moment from my past came flooding back in. More than anything else I wanted respect and I felt Simone was disrespecting me. All the years of never being heard or expressing myself exploded out of me. First, I screamed, and then that wasn't enough. I wanted so badly for him to get out of my car and give me space. He wasn't listening to me, and I hit him. I reached across to the passenger seat and hit him hard in the chest.

After that first strike, my fists continued to fly. In the process, my finger caught on his grandfather's gold cross necklace that he wore. It broke and flew down to his feet. As he bent to retrieve it, I ran out of the car and into the house. I was out of control, and so was Simone, who followed me inside and refused to leave. I called the police, who said they couldn't make Simone leave since he had been living in the house for the past seven months and that entitled him to stay.

I was devastated that they couldn't just make it happen. Who knows what those cops thought of me that night, but I was desperate and I needed support. Simone never left and we eventually made up, in just the same dynamic fashion that Tyler and I, always, would.

And that began the theme to our relationship.

Instead of living with someone who was sex-obsessed, it would now be all about money: as much as he could get and however he could get it, no matter the cost.

My Dream

I saw the lights as they passed on my left. I saw buildings and their structures, soft and glowing. I saw their flicker as they glazed my eyes. In my eyes, they turned in color. Left them grey and black. No sunshine shown. They were swirling in smoke falling towards darkness.

One day I saw ahead of me, left me staring into its magic. One day that I saw ahead of left me calm, quiet, undisturbed. Through the glass, fallen colors of earth warmed my heart. Blue, green, all pastels glazed my reflective eyes. When I opened my eyes before sleep vanished, doom appeared. I said, "Still?" and "This is what remains?" Into the grey I dove from the wreckage and copied following the path towards where my dream had been.

8/15/96

COSTA RICA

Simone and I fell into a routine of visiting each other in our respective cities, and all seemed to be going well. We considered ourselves to be dating, and I hoped exclusively, although I was never quite sure. Simone was a persuasive guy. High energy, captivating, entertaining, always on the verge of something big and great, he had the ability to make whoever he was around feel they were the only person in his world—except, of course, for the endless horde he communicated with via phone.

He was forever putting together some gig or event and talking about how many hundreds of thousands of dollars it was going to cost. But he appeared to do okay. He drove a CLS Mercedes-Benz, he lived in an opulent neighborhood with his family, and he moved in a tiny, well-connected circle in Toronto.

Our early fights aside, I felt like I was a part of something really great with him, and I hoped it would continue, though I often found myself in quieter moments when I was alone wrestling with how he fit into my desire for independence and freedom. Although I had needed Robert to climb out of the hellhole I was in with Tyler, I continued to suffer from our divorce. Why did splitting have to be so petty and nasty? If the point was to hurt the other person, job well done, I was permanently scarred.

I could live with my present-day conflicts and confusion.

Not too far from where I lived in Venice, I started working out daily at YAS, which stood for Yoga and Spinning. I loved the community of women who attended the classes. All of us were drawn to the teacher, a charismatic woman whose body and spirit radiated an enviable health, well-being, and balance. When she spoke of a YAS retreat focused on yoga and surfing in Costa Rica, I was immediately on board.

I had never been there, and it sounded wonderful. I asked my girlfriend Stephanie. We had been hanging out a lot more since I left Robert, and it turned out my timing was perfect. She was more than up for a girls' trip that was all about fitness and wellness. She said it was exactly what she needed at the moment.

Simone was in Toronto when Stephanie and I departed. I called him from the gate and we gushed about our love for each other. After saying goodbye, though, I had the feeling that I was disconnecting from him and the whole world. Our flight was long and then we had an equally long drive to Nosara, a beach town on the Pacific side of Costa Rica. Stephanie was excellent traveling company and I was glad she was with me. We stayed at a remote private residence located up the mountain from town, in what appeared to be the middle of the jungle.

In addition to a main house, the property featured an assortment of bungalows, but Stephanie and I quickly chose the large room in the main house. A dozen other women were also on the retreat; it seemed like a good group. Stephanie had confided that she needed some time away from her relationship. She had been doing some heavy-duty soul-searching of late, and this trip to a beautiful and isolated spot where she knew no one and nothing more was required of her than to look inside herself was just the medicine she craved.

I remember listening to her story during our drive and offering her the softest, most understanding smile I could conjure, saying, "Same here. Everything you just said and more."

She had always encouraged me to live my best life since meeting me when I was still with Tyler and in fact helping me to escape his dastardly clutches. She was as close as I had to a sister, and I knew that I could always count on hearing her cheer for me from the sidelines. I looked forward to doing the same for her on this trip.

The daily schedule was full of activities. We started out by hitting the beach. Stephanie surfed while I watched from the safety of the beach, happy to sunbathe and not worry about sharks, stingrays, or other creatures beneath the surface that fed my still-present phobia. The next day we hit the trails on ATVs, something I had never done. As we raced along, I felt free. In the morning and that night, the sounds of the jungle were an exotic symphony.

"How do you feel?" I asked Stephanie as we got into our respective beds and turned off the light.

"Great. Wonderful. Calm," she said. "How about you?"

I took a deep breath, listened to the chatter of monkeys outside, and stared into the dark.

"For the first time in forever, I'm really excited to get up tomorrow morning and see what's gonna happen," I said.

Little did I suspect I would almost die, again.

THE JUNGLE

Not everyone on the trip wanted to ride horses, but six of us ladies headed out in the morning and met our trail guide by the side of the main highway that went into town. The horses were lined up behind him. We got out and walked up to meet him while eyeing the horses and deciding which one to ride. We spoke of our experience, if any, riding. Stephanie had grown up with horses, and even though I could close my eyes and picture my Kodak disaster in Guatemala, I considered myself pretty good, and at the least, comfortable on a horse. Stephanie and I even rode on occasion in LA.

After each of us got our horse, we ventured off into the jungle. We followed our guide, who didn't speak English very well, down the trail paths and across three rivers, until we arrived at his family home's coffee orchard. After serving us a delicious home-cooked lunch, he gave a tour of their coffee-growing and -making operations. He explained the process and then served us coffee. It was like no coffee I had ever tasted: thick, aromatic, strong, and with a flavor that wafted up from the steam coming from the cup, exploding on my taste buds.

My thank-you to him and his family was profuse and heartfelt. Sitting there was like having stepped into a real-life storybook. The beautiful, exotic nature of the setting was a vacation wrapped inside our retreat. It reminded me of my time in the Australian rainforest, like the present was deeper, more vivid, and richer for the experience, almost hyperreal.

I got a hug from Stephanie, who felt the same. But I was feeling a sense of liberation unlike any time before. I had been invited to many events and retreats over the years but never gone. I was too caught up in what I figured my image needed to be. It was difficult to feel like I might be recognized by people who knew me when I didn't know them. It was weird to catch people staring at me and sometimes hear them talking about me. Even if they weren't, it was easy to imagine they were, and of course I imagined whatever they were saying was judgmental. So why be in that position on a retreat that was supposed to be a relaxing escape?

Although I had agreed to the retreat as soon as I heard about it, I had to talk myself past the fact I would be with other women and feel vulnerable in such proximity. My issues around trust (or lack of it) and insecurity fed into my sense that no one really cared for me, and all that was amplified by the feeling that I would be on display. If not for the fondness I had for the community at YAS, I probably would have talked myself out of going to Costa Rica and missed out.

After we got back on our horses, I was feeling rather proud of myself and confident for not missing out, for being on the jungle trail in the open air atop this magnificent animal, for being connected to nature and myself. I took a deep breath and felt my lungs expand with the enervating thrill of being alive and in the moment. Past the guide's home, as we headed back, we went up the embankment and over to a waterfall, where we stopped to take a swim, sit below the falls, and enjoy the scenery.

Having been told the day before we were going to make this scenic stop, all of us had brought or worn a bathing suit. I had my bikini on underneath my deerskin riding pants and a long-sleeve hooded T-shirt that said YAS. I also had my riding gloves with me but not my helmet. I didn't think I'd need one.

After we finished enjoying the falls, we got back on our horses and headed back up another embankment to the next river to cross. This time, I led the group. The ride was transcendental, a total release where I was free and in nature, seeing and feeling a part of everything, grateful and exhilarated for being present and alive. The wind was in my face and my skin tingled; every nerve wired into the moment and danced with electricity.

My horse and I hit the river and trudged through cold water. Then we popped out and both of us shook and flung water everywhere.

Every cell in my body was screaming go! Go! *Go!*

I kicked my horse into a gallop as I had done all day, which I knew was pushing it as far as my riding ability went. I couldn't help myself. Even as we galloped and I heard a voice in my head warn, "You're pushing it," I didn't listen. I wanted to taste, see, and feel every drop of existence here, the quiet and stillness of the morning and night and the thrills of being outdoors. Every so often I turned to look back at our guide and Stephanie and the others. I flashed them a smile.

I was still leading the group when we came up onto the second embankment. I kicked my horse and let loose the same adrenaline-filled cry of enthusiasm I had done all day at moments like this. It was a sound that both humans and horses understood, a sound that said, "Let's go! Let's charge into the fun." The group behind me echoed my soaring spirit, and we were all a cohesive unit of souls flying over the ground in tune with the driving rhythm of horse hooves pummeling the ground.

And that's when, for a brief second, I saw it.

The trail was about ten to twelve feet wide, but there was a small hole, about half a foot across, toward the middle, and my horse's front left hoof went straight into it, causing him to lose his balance. He fell to the left and both of us went down. I hit the ground first and all sixteen hundred pounds of horse followed on top of me. My left leg bore the brunt of it as we slid about twelve feet in deceleration.

When it happened, Stephanie was behind me. She jerked her horse to the right and watched horrified as it happened, actually flipping off her own horse and turning back to watch since she didn't have enough time to rein her horse to a halt. The woman behind her had to swerve and jump over us, as well. Others also stopped or managed to get around us before stopping without getting hurt. There could have been quite a serious pileup and chain-reaction disaster, but remarkably and thankfully, no one else was hurt.

I was on the ground in a twisted heap, looking up toward the sky. My neck was bent all the way to the side, almost touching my shoulder, and I was listening to the leaves rustle above me. For a moment, everyone's voices and all the other sounds of the world around me seemed to disappear except for the rustling. It was so quiet and peaceful for a split second, and then the chaos came flooding in.

Am I paralyzed? I wondered.

My brain, fueled by adrenaline and shock, raced. I was terrified. And scared. I was astounded to even be alive, since I wasn't wearing a helmet. It was an absolute fucking miracle, no doubt about it. But was I paralyzed? I was afraid to find out. Then I realized I could try to wiggle my toes. I had no real idea what state my neck or back were in and I knew it was best to not move much of anything in case I was in a fragile state and the slightest twinge might produce serious, lasting damage. But I figured I could at least wiggle my toes and not make the situation worse.

I took a deep breath and tried. And they wiggled. Barely. But it was proof enough that I would be able to still walk.

I don't know what I have done to deserve this favor, but thank you, God, I thought.

Then, I knew the horse's weight had been massive on me, and I worried that I could have some sort of internal damage that I couldn't readily see.

I had no idea how we were going to get out of there. We were completely in the middle of the jungle. Me, with five other women and a guide who spoke no English. No road nearby, no cell phone, and even if we'd had a phone, no one knew the retreat's number.

Then, pain hit, and it was excruciating. It was most intense in my left hip, and I was convinced it was broken. Between that and my fear of internal bleeding, I wasn't sure whether I should move from where I had fallen. Neither were my companions. The women were frantic and unsure about what to do. We were in the jungle, with three rivers to cross and three more trails to travel along before we got to a road.

I called over Stephanie and two others, who knelt down next to me. For some reason, I felt as if the pain had shocked me into a hyperclarity.

"Don't move me," I said. "I don't know if it's safe yet."

"Okay," Stephanie said.

Then I had an idea. I said, "Take your water bottles to the river and fill them up. The water is ice cold. If we can soak my leg in the cold, maybe the swelling will stop and maybe go down." I was desperate to try anything as soon as possible, as I knew I had incurred a lot of trauma to my body and it would, most likely, be reacting soon.

A few of the women went down to get the water while the others tried to talk with our guide. His young daughter, who had come along with us after lunch, rode back to their home to gather materials that would help them build a stretcher that would enable them to carry me out of there. My brain was going one hundred miles per hour. There was nothing I could do except analyze the situation and my place in it. This was my nightmare of participating in a group. I was helpless, vulnerable, and reliant on others. I was fully exposed and couldn't pretend otherwise.

I hadn't been showboating, but I had been pushing myself and my horse to the limit. My inner voice had warned me, along the way, saying, "You're pushing it." And now this outrageous situation. Had I gotten what I deserved? Was this payback from the Universe? A message or lesson? And if so, what was it?

TREE OF LIFE

Time passed, and we were still on the trail. I hadn't moved. We were waiting for the guide's young daughter to return with items to build a makeshift stretcher. I was unsure of this idea, but I had no choice.

"We're too deep in the jungle for a helicopter even if we could reach one," Stephanie said.

"Not close to any roads," our guide said in broken English.

His concern looked like it had been chiseled deep into his face.

"We must carry you out," he said.

"We don't have a choice," Stephanie said. "But we'll get you out. You're going to be okay. I promise."

Finally, the guide's daughter returned and she brought a bundle of scarves and fabrics they had in their home. The girls started to weave them together, and used two large tree branches they had found, each about five inches in diameter, as the side poles. After it was assembled, I watched one of them get into it to test the weight. She even thrashed around a bit to make sure it was secure. It held her perfectly. Everyone congratulated one another. Getting me into it without too much pain was another challenge that had to be handled with delicacy and care. I also had to let go and trust.

It was just us women with our one male guide to carry me out of the jungle. The ladies rallied together, got me on the stretcher, hoisted me up, and started to walk. I had no idea what happened to the horses.

"Are you okay?" they asked periodically.

"How are you doing, Mena?"

Strangely, I couldn't remember the last time anybody had asked how I was doing in a nonwork situation. On the set, sure. *How you doing, Mena? Holding up?* These circumstances were drastically different. I was aware that if my body was dipped down on my left side, the most intense pain would shoot up it, like lightning bolts shooting out from my hip. I was convinced it was broken. But the trail was rutted, the women were doing their best to carry a little more than one hundred extra pounds through the jungle, up and down hills and through water, on a makeshift stretcher, and I just kept quiet. At various times, I thought I might pass out. It might have been easier.

At one point, as we fought our way through the cold, waist-high water, I noticed that a large bird—an eagle—was flying in a line above us. It was beautiful to see, and I found comfort in watching its graceful, attentive flight. I took it as a positive sign and lost myself in this unique perspective. Instead of staring straight down the trail or looking side to side, I could look only straight up at the treetops and, beyond them, the birds and the sky. It was a window into the infinite, the source of everything, where the planet began with a bang and to where all things great and small traced the miracle and mystery of existence. I saw nothing and everything, and despite being in this state where I couldn't move, and perhaps because of some delirium from the unremitting pain, I felt my soul leave my body and take flight and soar with the eagle.

Someone said that six hours had passed by the time they got me on the stretcher and took to the trail. I had no idea of time anymore. Stephanie stayed by my side through it all. After what seemed like forever, we reached the initial bank we had set out on earlier in the day. It was the closest to the main road but still remote. The ladies laid me down on the ground, underneath a large and beautiful tree, and took a breather. They were wrecked. I felt bad about ruining the outing, inconveniencing everyone, and everything.

The sun was starting to set. One of the girls knew the route to get back to the main house we were staying in. Undeterred by our own lack of transportation, she scrambled out to the road, flagged down a passing motorcyclist, and told him of what had happened, and he took her back to the house to notify the owners and get help.

After she left, I didn't see Stephanie and panicked. I needed to ask her a question, and I was upset about it. It turned out she was down by the river, trying to gather her wits after hours of this craziness. She had thought I'd died when I fell, then she had the anxiety of getting me out of the jungle, and then she discovered the tree they had laid me down under was known as the "Tree of Life." It was all too much for her; she needed a moment.

"What's up, honey?" she said, hurrying to my side after hearing me call her name in a stressed-out voice.

"I have to pee," I said. "I have to go to the bathroom."

Desperate and embarrassed, I needed her to tell me what to do even though I already knew the answer. I was in such excruciating pain, I couldn't move at all, let alone stand and walk somewhere looking for privacy.

"It's okay, babe," she said. "Just do it. It's okay. Just go."

Staring up at the Tree of Life, I let go and peed all over myself.

More time went by until the woman who'd hitchhiked on the motorcycle came back with the woman from the house and another man in a tiny truck. I heard their voices from the road as they discussed how to load me into the back. I immediately sensed it wasn't going to work, and it didn't. The space was too small. I was only able to fit if I squished, and I wasn't able to move anything without severe pain. They tried once but I let out a blood-curdling scream and it was a no-go.

Darkness had blanketed the jungle by the time two young doctors from a local clinic knelt by my side and asked how I was doing. Another six hours had passed while I lay under the canopy, and I was in pain, had peed my pants, had eaten nothing but a Clif Bar Stephanie had in her bag, and was probably dehydrated, and I was still pretty terrified of the damage I'd done to myself. But I wasn't paralyzed and I hadn't died from internal bleeding, yet, as I still worried I would. I was surrounded by a group of remarkable women. I was grateful to be alive.

"We will get you to our clinic," one doctor said.

"I think I have a broken hip," I said.

"We will see."

These two doctors gave me the sense they had the situation under control. They weren't panicked, which calmed me for the first time in the twelve hours since the accident happened. After a cursory check, they lifted me up and put me in the back of their off-road ambulance. It wasn't an easy fit, but it was better than the first truck, so I bit the bullet and hoped for the best.

THE RESCUE

Their ambulance was a rigged VW bus that had a sort of snorkel snout attached to one side of it so that it was able to drive through the rivers. Later, Stephanie said we drove through the river, in at least five feet of water, to get out of the jungle. The trip to their clinic wasn't long. It was across the street from the local soccer field and park area. Amid a chaotic bustle of activity, the doctors got me into an examining room and proceeded to assess my injuries.

As they used huge bandage scissors to cut off my deerskin britches, I said so long to the nine hundred dollars I had wasted on those pants. Because I had told them of the pain I had in my hip and how I was sure it was broken, they wanted a visual. One of the doctors felt my abdomen. I freaked and blurted out my worry of internal bleeding.

"I don't think so," the doctor said. "Your abdomen would be distended and you're not displaying that symptom." I felt so relieved to hear that.

But to be sure, they were going to send me to San José for X-rays and an MRI if that was also necessary. Their tiny clinic didn't have such equipment. The helicopter was already on its way, they said. As we waited, they finished their exam. When word came that the helicopter was arriving, they wheeled me outside and across the street to the park where it had landed. A huge crowd watched. From my limited, flat view on top of the gurney, I wondered aloud if it was that big of a deal. Much later, Stephanie would inform me that there had been a soccer game taking place, and with the field being the best and largest spot to land, they interrupted the game to load me in. Quite a "halftime"!

Nonetheless, the doctors explained, this was exciting for the town since the majority of the time they saw this kind of activity it was because of who was being cared for. "You're a white lady, a gringa," one of the doctors said. "The people who live here can't afford something like this."

Running a hand over his face and through his hair, he and his partner explained that many of the local women traveled for miles in the backs of flatbed trucks when they went into labor. They told me how people with serious illnesses that couldn't be treated here did the same thing, and how many of them over the years had succumbed while making the long trip in the backs of trucks and cars on their way to get assistance. My heart broke listening about this very different reality for the people who lived locally, many of whom seemed to be staring at me as I was wheeled to the helicopter.

They were like me. Young people, teenagers, mothers with children— whoever had been in the park or nearby. I was upset these doctors didn't have the most basic X-ray machines or other up-to-date equipment. I wanted to make it my mission to help them in some way down the line, but I didn't because I just didn't know how.

I heard Stephanie complaining to someone who had said they didn't have enough room for her to accompany me. The helicopter could fit only so many of us. I was transferred onto a stretcher and loaded into the back, where a nurse sat next to me, secured me in place, and started taking my blood pressure and other vitals. Stephanie was incredibly upset about being left behind, as was I. We didn't want to be separated. I was hurt. We were in a foreign country, and I didn't want to leave her alone. I was about to chopper off to another city. And where in that other city? I had never been anywhere else before in this country.

I handed Stephanie my phone and told her how to unlock it. I needed her to call my mom and Simone.

"Tell them what happened and where I'm going," I said.

"Okay," she said, wearily.

"I love you," I said.

"I love you, too," she said.

As they loaded me into the helicopter, I felt like a little girl and was terrified to go onward by myself. I thought so deeply, *I want my mom.*

IN NEED

My head was completely locked into place. They had put headphones on me to help drown out the noise of the chopper, and as we started to make our way through the night to San José, I began to settle in as much as I could, knowing it would be a little bit before we would arrive. Then, I realized the music playing in my headphones was from Pink Floyd's *The Wall*. Oh, how random. I couldn't help but laugh. My fear and stress had risen to such a level that it was all I could do.

The trip to the hospital in San José didn't seem to take long. I was wheeled into the ER and put through a battery of X-rays and exams. I waited anxiously for the results, and then the doctor came back in and told me that nothing was broken or bleeding. I couldn't believe it. I hadn't been wearing a helmet. I had sixteen hundred pounds of horse fall on me. Both of us sliding down the trail. I should have been dead. And now the doctor was telling me that nothing was broken, not even a hairline fracture. I didn't have any internal bleeding, I was just severely bruised.

"Really?" I asked.

"You are very fortunate," he said.

Shocked, I tried to process this news in the context of still suffering the most physical pain and anguish that I had ever experienced.

"I want you to stay the night," he said.

Before the doctor left, I asked if they had food and pain medication like aspirin or ibuprofen on the floor where I was being moved. He assured me

I would get everything I needed. I was worried. It was late and I was absolutely starving. "Not a problem," he said.

Except it was.

After I was taken to another floor and given a bed, I asked the nurses for two things, food and soap. I wanted to eat and wash the scratches and cuts all over my body. I was told the food was not available, the kitchen was closed, and I was devastated. Weren't people supposed to be cared for in this hospital? The nurses left my room shaking their heads.

I seemed to be the only one on the floor. I waited for soap, but nothing came. I was so hungry, and so tired at the same time, but I at least wanted to clean myself. My pants had been cut off me, making me feel grateful for my somewhat decent bikini underneath, and I was still covered in mud. I needed to clean the wounds I'd gotten. I waited until I couldn't take it anymore. Slowly, carefully, and painfully, I shifted toward the side of the bed, dropped my feet, and stood up. I stood still for a moment, acclimating to the pain and waiting for my head to clear. I took hold of my IV stand, which was still attached to my arm, and, as I wheeled it next to me, shuffled into the hallway.

As I poked my head into the corridor, I turned into a woman on a mission. I felt a surge of adrenaline over how wrong this situation felt. Two nurses saw me from the nurses' station and looked up, surprised. They had been chatting, laughing. I wanted to apologize for interrupting their good time, sarcastically, of course.

"Soap?" I asked. "Do you have soap? *Jabón*?" I wasn't even sure of the Spanish word for it, I just felt so desperate to get it that I tried anything.

One of them finally walked around and came up to me with a small, travel-size bar. I thanked her and walked back to my room. Once back there, I realized I wanted out of this place. As soon as possible. I was starving, exhausted, dirty, in pain. I noted how the pain that had overwhelmed me for the past eighteen hours and still throbbed with each beat of my heart did not even rank atop my list of complaints. Sleep. Nourishment. Familiar surroundings. Healing. Normalcy. I wanted out of there.

I remembered I had the number for the owner of the house where we were staying for the retreat. I found it and called. The owner picked up right away, and listened patiently while I listed all of my frustration, desperation, and fear, poured out in a frantic plea to pick me up as soon as possible.

"I will do better on my own," I said. "I just need to get to a hotel. I'm okay; I just have to get out of here."

She understood. She said she had a driver in San José who would take me to a hotel she knew of and would contact him immediately. She gave me his number, too; just in case I didn't hear from him.

"He will call you," she said.

"Thank you," I said, sobbing.

I was getting closer to getting out and being able to fall asleep and forget this whole day had ever happened.

I went into the bathroom with my small bar of soap and got ready to shower. I wondered why I'd had to fight so fiercely for the soap and also why they couldn't even find a package of crackers. It was strange they didn't have anything and didn't even try to find something. The hot water felt like heaven against my body. I took a deep breath and pulled out the IV. I held my arm above my head to slow the flow of blood.

After I finished cleaning myself, I slipped back into the clothes I had on when I arrived: my bikini, T-shirt, and socks. With my ass pretty much hanging out the back of my hospital gown, I grabbed my backpack and walked through the doorway and into the hallway, ending at the nurses' station, and told them that I wanted to leave. They said I couldn't go. I didn't understand why, and our inability to communicate clearly didn't help clarify the situation. I was down to the last few strands of sanity before I broke. I knew that all I needed to do was sign a waiver taking my own life into my hands and that would give me the authority to leave on my own. I had learned this when Robert refused immediate surgery on his arm to wait for an expert. I had no idea what they were implying by being so resistant.

Then the elevator doors opened. A man stepped out, looked at all of us, and then at me.

"Mena Suvari?" he asked.

"Yes!" I screamed. "I want to go. Now, please."

For some reason, he walked past me. Perhaps to avoid a fracas with the nurses, who no longer appeared friendly. I stepped into the elevator and implored him to get in with me. We had to go. Now! The doors closed just as the nurses reached us and we landed on the lobby level, my driver and me in a T-shirt, bikini bottoms, and dirty socks. I walked through the waiting area, past dozens of freestanding chairs, and straight up to the main doors. They were locked.

"What the fuck?" I said, exasperated.

I tried several other doors.

All were locked.

When I looked back over my shoulder, I saw a group of men huddled near the elevator. They looked toward me, gestured, talked among themselves, and appeared to wait for me to walk back to the elevator. Once again I asked why I couldn't leave without getting a reply. Exhausted and defeated, I shuffled over to one of the metal chairs and sat down.

One of the men—I assumed they were doctors, but they could have been nurses, orderlies, or security guards—came over and said I needed to go into an office. I followed him into a room with chairs opposite various cubicles. After waiting several minutes, a woman entered and said I couldn't leave until I paid. That's what this was about? Dealing with a bill?

Somehow I knew all my insurance information and credit card had been given to the hospital ahead of my arrival, which I explained, adding that this was a mistake on their part. The woman opposite me argued otherwise and even seemed to scoff at my explanation, making me feel like I was trying to cheat them. I lost it.

"Let me ask you this: How was your day?" I snapped. "Did your pen run out of ink? Was your coffee cold? Were you late to a meeting? Because I almost fucking died today. And I'm in a foreign country. And I don't know where I am. And I want to get out of here. And you're telling me I need to pay when I have already given all my information." I knew this was their mistake, but I was so shocked by the dismissiveness.

Without saying a word, she got up and left the room. A few minutes later, she returned and stood by the door.

"You are right," she said. "You may go."

The driver was waiting for me in the lobby. I followed him out into the parking lot and over to his VW bus. I stepped gently over the dark pavement in my soiled socks. I had no clue who this man was or where we were going at this late hour, but I got in his bus and sunk into the back seat with no more will to fight. I only wanted this day to be over and the next one to be better.

CRIES HEARD

tried to get as comfortable as possible by stretching out and leaning against the window on the left. I gazed out the window, looking deep into the night, with all the neon lights of San José shimmering across the landscape. I had no idea where I was or what this part of the city looked like. It was so dark out on the road. I felt awkward, again. Another continuous part to this wild adventure. How had I found myself, in the middle of the night, half-naked in the back of a van driven by a man I'd never met? The driver didn't say much, but I knew he was sympathetic. After twenty to thirty minutes, we pulled into a hotel parking lot and he stopped by the front door. After helping me inside, he said that he would meet me in this same spot later in the morning to bring me to the airport, where I would fly back to Nosara. I walked into the hotel and over to the man waiting behind the front desk. I asked if they had a room and he smiled.

"Of course. We have been expecting you."

"By any chance, do you have a toothbrush?" I asked.

I wanted so many things at that moment—sleep, food, to get back to my group in Nosara—but more than anything I wanted to get clean, to somehow wash this nightmare from my skin.

"Yes, yes, of course," he said, before offering me a small, sealed, disposable beauty kit that included a toothbrush, toothpaste, a mini-razor and shaving cream, Q-tips, shampoo, and soap.

I was on the verge of tears. The relief I felt was like a gentle massage. The tension that had held me together and kept me awake and upright began to dissipate.

"This is so wonderful," I said. "Thank you so much. Do you have any food?"

"Our room service is twenty-four hours," he said.

It really upset me to know there was such a disparity. I wondered where I was that had these amenities that were not available at the local hospital. And why didn't the hospital have the ability to provide soap and food? By the time I got to my room, I quit asking questions and let myself simply be. I had no more fight in me, no more energy to process anything other than washing up, getting into bed, taking immense pleasure in the thick, clean white bed linens, and falling into a deep sleep as soon as my head hit the pillow.

The morning arrived in the blink of an eye. Everything ached but not as severely as before. I ordered breakfast and called the house to let them know how I was doing and to arrange to get back there. After working out arrangements for a flight back to Nosara, I asked to speak with Stephanie. When she heard my voice, the poor girl broke down. All the emotions she'd held back crashed through the paper-thin walls. I understood and cried some myself.

"I have to tell you that I reached your mother earlier this morning," she said.

"What happened?" I asked, eager to hear, then was fascinated that her recollection, strange as it was, seemed to be real.

"She answered the phone right away," Stephanie said. "It was like she heard your cry all the way from the jungle."

I listened, feeling surprised.

"She said she knew something was wrong with you but she wasn't sure what it was. She had a feeling that someone was going to call. She had woken up earlier than normal, made her bed, placed her phone on it, and waited for it to ring."

"And you told her what happened?"

"Yes. I told her that you were okay and flying back to Nosara today. She was so grateful to hear you were all right."

"You are amazing," I said. "Thank you."

Before leaving the hotel that afternoon, I stopped in a gift shop and bought thank-you presents—pretty little necklaces and earrings—for the five women who saved my life. At the airport, a small single-engine propellor plane waited to take me back to Nosara. Getting into the two-seater made me nervous, but I was compelled to go with it. Watching the pilot walk around to the front of the plane and spin the rotor blade to get the engine going seemed surreal, but I needed to get back and so many people had pitched in to make these arrangements that I swallowed my anxiety.

Once in the air, though, it all made sense. We climbed above the city, sounding like a giant flying insect, and made our way west toward the coast. I had almost died the day before, and by all rights, without a helmet, I should not have survived, yet here I was, soaring through the sky and feeling electric because of it. The beauty of the landscape below was breathtaking. Lush forests. Waterfalls. Rivers. I felt like I was having an out-of-body experience. I was simultaneously above the world and in it, seeing my place without seeing myself. No judgment. Just being.

I had been given life.

But why? Why was I still here?

I didn't feel like I deserved it.

It was a gift.

Through so many hardships, through so many times of coming just up to the brink of death, my life was always spared.

I felt mystified by it all, but now with a deeper sense of connection and gratitude than I'd ever had before.

GRATITUDE

When we touched down on the tarmac in Nosara, the doctor who had treated me the night before was waiting to greet me. He wanted to see for himself that I was okay, he explained. I thanked him and expressed my appreciation in every way I could think of—in English, in broken Spanish, with smiles and hugs. Nothing felt like enough.

On the drive back to the house, I was hit by a feeling that I shouldn't be there. The reality of what I had just survived was sinking in more and more; I felt half out of my body and was trying to reconnect with this existence again. But I wasn't sure how to simply go back to the house, where it felt like I needed to just pick up from where our glorious retreat had come to a crashing halt for me. The mood had changed. I was eager to reconnect with everyone, yet something felt off.

I tried to block that out as we arrived at the house. I walked in and dropped my backpack. When I found Stephanie in the backyard garden, we hugged as if I had been gone a year, not a day. She was still pretty emotional and having a hard time processing everything that had happened. And she wasn't the only one. She told me that some of the other women on the retreat felt like they were hearing too much about the accident. They felt bad, but they also wanted to move on and continue with the trip as planned.

"They don't want to deal and I've been dealing with it on my own and . . ." Stephanie put her hands over her eyes and rubbed the tears before they had a chance to fall. "It's just been hard. I'm sorry."

202

I hugged her.

"I'm sorry, too."

We offered each other much-needed support. But I had a hard time accepting the attitude the other women had expressed to Stephanie. After a few hours there, I picked up on the tense dynamic and told Stephanie that I sensed the resentment boiling beneath the smiles and hugs. However, I had no energy or interest in confronting other people's issues. I was the one who'd been involved in the accident and suffered the cuts and injuries. I felt horrible that this all had happened, but no matter how much gratitude I expressed, it still felt like it would never communicate how much I never wanted any of this to even happen.

Late that afternoon, I walked out to the back and found a little overlook area where I could sit and be with myself. I felt like I was on acid. Everything within my perception felt tangible, even my existence.

I tried to be still and meditate. I was sorry if I'd ruined the day and night, upset everyone's sleep, and cast a pall over their morning yoga and surfing. I was also sorry for the ways it deeply affected my friend. Stephanie was really unmoored. She had come to work on herself, and I had blown that plan to smithereens.

The sun shifted and began to sink beneath the treetops. I looked out over the Costa Rican jungle and the dense greenery as it sloped all the way down to the beach. Thoughts and emotions swirled through my head. I seemed to experience everything all at once. Calm, anger, confusion, heaviness, gratitude, pain, sorrow, isolation, connectedness, and eventually the lightness I had experienced earlier in the little plane that had ferried me back from the hospital.

I thought about the eagle that had followed me as the women carried me through the jungle on the makeshift stretcher. Later that night, I was browsing in the house's library and found a book titled *Animal Speak: The Spiritual and Magical Power of Creatures Great and Small*. I turned to the page on eagles and read this majestic bird was long considered a messenger of God.

It made sense to me. When I was being carried through the rivers and down the trails, this great creature who symbolized eternal life had flown with strength and grace directly in line with us. It was a message to me, and I was only just waking up to it. I would need much more time before I would understand the meaning and know how to act on it. But I was a survivor. Why couldn't I see that? Why did it, continuously, take me so long to listen?

From the day my mother, newly pregnant with me, fell down the stairs and feared she lost me, to this very day, and through the umpteen close calls I had in between (a terrible crash I took when I was seven, a thirty-foot fall off a cliff when we lived in St. John, slicing my vein on a coral reef, causing profuse bleeding, and more), I was meant to live, to be here, to be alive— and loved. The Universe was showing me how much it loved me. I just had to quit doubting it, quit fighting it, and learn how to love myself.

... Look at us, hear us ... Heart of Heaven,
Heart of Earth ... May the people have peace, much peace,
and may they be happy; and give us good life ... grandmother
of the sun, grandmother of the light, let there be dawn,
and let the light come! ...

• Mayan Dawn Prayer
Tenth Century

LOVE AND LOSS

Stephanie and I finished out the trip in Costa Rica glued to each other's side before returning to Los Angeles. Back home, the dance was a familiar one of reconnecting with Simone, my agent, and my friends; filling time; and waiting for something to happen.

When Simone said he and some friends had work in Jamaica, I went along to be with him and, as we vowed, to make our own memories together. Mission accomplished. We lounged at the beach, frolicked in the water, ate the best food, and made love nonstop in the little house where we stayed. I called it magical. Simone said it was love. Whatever, I didn't want it to end.

Neither did I want to be apart from Simone. Soon after getting back home, I was packing for a trip to Toronto so I could spend more time with him. Being in Jamaica had inspired me to reassess our relationship. Though our fights in the beginning had been rough and nasty, we had settled into an easier, more considerate, and loving place. I was also more settled within myself and ready for a commitment.

Apparently Simone felt the same way. One night, as we stood on the balcony in the amazing hotel suite where I stayed in Toronto, he knelt down and proposed. He gave me a small black box. Inside was the largest diamond ring I had ever seen. Amazed, surprised, and excited, I figured I was ready this time. I was of the so-called age and eager to settle down. I adored his family and even imagined starting one of our own. The timing hadn't been right when I was with Robert, but I thought I was ready and Simone gave me the impression that he was the right one.

Simone and I shared a taste for the finer things, which I found sexy about him, but this ring was way too much. Never had I pictured a ring like that on my finger. It was so unbelievably gorgeous, but the stone was so large, too large for my taste, and seemingly way too large for his bank account. I wondered how he could have afforded it. I couldn't have afforded it.

I ignored the red flag. I was proof that love is blind. And indeed, I would commit in saying yes to Simone and committing to a future that would prove to be a very bitter fantasy. Once engaged, though, I focused on the wedding.

Both of us wanted a fairy-tale wedding in Italy. It had to be in Italy. We wanted to go there and hunt for the perfect locations for the ceremony and reception. Because Simone spoke Italian fluently, I left him in charge of organizing everything there. I assumed responsibility for the invitations and everything else that could be handled in the US.

Eager, and in retrospect pathetically desperate to nail down this part of my life, I ignored more red flags: I was paying for everything, and I couldn't afford it.

I should have realized this when I took out a twenty-thousand-dollar loan against my pension. But I didn't. And neither Simone nor I thought about scaling back our nuptials or any other plans.

One afternoon Simone and I were eating lunch at a restaurant in downtown LA when someone seated nearby overheard us talking about real estate and mentioned that he knew of a penthouse coming up for sale in a nearby building. He said he could show it to us because he was a Realtor himself and also happened to live on the same floor in the building.

Simone and I traded glances. I was interested. I loved looking at properties, and downtown LA lofts were all the rage. But I quietly and discreetly said I wanted my friend Sigal to show it to us and represent us should we be interested.

"She's a Realtor," I said. "And she's my best friend."

"So is this guy," Simone said. "We're here. He can show it to us now. We don't know when Sigal will be available."

"I want to be loyal to her," I said.

"It's just so convenient to do it now," he said.

Simone and I started to argue. He didn't find any issue in working with this guy who we didn't know and who was trying to capitalize on having overheard our conversation.

"I don't know this guy," I said. "But more importantly, Sigal is my friend."

I wanted to be loyal to her, but that seemed the furthest thing from Simone's mind.

To avoid any more conflict, I reluctantly gave in to Simone. We saw the unit, which was a large artist's loft, with tall ceilings, floor-to-ceiling windows, and lots of room. Both of us were impressed. It needed a lot of work, but Simone started coming up with ideas, some practical, some incredibly extravagant, like installing a Ferrari bar. I feigned interest even though I had no intention of purchasing the condo.

However, a couple days later, I did mention the place to Sigal on the phone and, as I suspected, she was upset that we hadn't called her to see it. She felt like it was a betrayal. I agreed with her, but she pushed the point to an extreme, and suddenly she was insulting Simone. What she said may have been truthful, but I took offense. I was talking to her from inside a studio where I was doing a photo shoot with a magazine that wanted to show off my engagement ring, and I noticed people looking at me. I stepped outside and found myself screaming at her as cars whizzed by on busy La Brea Avenue. I felt sick but unmoored as both of us got nastier by the second.

"Well, have a great life," I finally snapped.

"You, too!" she said, and hung up.

I stood on the sidewalk and imagined the world swallowing me up. I had just lost my best friend. I was sick and the whole thing made me sicker as time passed. Sigal was the only person I'd ever let know my true self. Soon after getting to know each other, we had bonded over trauma. She was the only one I ever let know the details of my life with Tyler, and even then I was too ashamed to tell her everything. Once, while we were out to lunch, I tried but my throat closed up. I couldn't get it out.

So after our blowout, I knew I would be lost without her, not only suddenly being without my best friend and confidant, but also losing a guiding light. I should have apologized. Pride kept me from making that call. I had to learn my lessons the hard way, the hardest one being that the more I looked for truths about my life, the more I ignored those right in front of me.

FEELING ALONE

S uccess in Hollywood made it easy to push the trauma and damage of my past into the background and pretend it didn't affect me. My life as an actress was too fabulous for such ugliness. Instead of doing the work necessary to reconcile and understand how to use all the advantages I had been afforded to help myself heal and become the best version of myself possible, I took the easy path and bought into the image the magazines, TV shows, and paparazzi had created for me. I was exceptional, a star, special—too special, in fact, to have problems.

I told myself the stories I told others and believed them. Why not? Although others didn't know me, they admired my work and professed to admire me, too. The same was true at photo shoots and in meetings. People told me that I looked fantastic, oh so beautiful. They asked if I wanted anything—coffee, water, soda, something to eat. Journalists wanted to know what was in my purse and on my playlist. I'd been paid $1 million for a film and another $800,000 to promote a beauty company. The attention was all on me, and I loved it. I couldn't do anything wrong.

Or so I told myself.

My accountant informed me I could no longer afford my Venice house and needed to downsize. I was able to sell before the 2008 crash, but managed to only break even. Unable to ask my ex–best friend Sigal for real estate advice, I signed papers on a beautiful, modern loft near Mid-City. Simone moved in and we continued to plan our wedding. Our choices were all top of the line and extravagant, causing me to flinch each time I heard the cost, but I never said no. I wanted a magical wedding in Italy.

Before we moved out of my Venice house, Simone and I bickered more than ever. I didn't think the business opportunities and music festivals he was always putting together were coming through, not in a way that stopped the flow from my bank account. Later on, Simone would admit his businesses were in the red and his personal account had a negative balance. But I needed him to step up before then, and I didn't feel like he did, not in the way I thought someone who could afford a massive diamond ring should have.

When he suggested loaning out my car to create a new revenue stream, I wanted to pull my hair out in frustration. This was so typical of Simone. It was his great idea, but the car was in my name and the liability would be all mine. I began to feel like he was about only his survival, getting whatever he could at other people's expense, including mine.

Communication between us worsened. Many times I couldn't wrap my head around his train of thought. I felt like he was always trying to twist and deceive and make me feel stupid, which I wasn't. I was, in fact, struggling to hang on to what I knew was right and proper, or what I thought I knew, because I was constantly having to convince myself that I wasn't going crazy. In that respect, I came to see too many similarities in our relationship to the dynamic I'd had with Tyler, and that frightened me.

One day we got into a massive fight and he left. I wanted him to leave and was relieved when he drove away. I fell onto the sofa, alone, drained, scared, and unnerved. My beautiful home that I could no longer afford was haunted; I was convinced that our fighting had filled the house with bad energy. Simone and I had been watching TV one night and heard loud, hard footsteps in our bedroom upstairs. I paused the TV and the steps were even clearer. Another time, my cousin and her girlfriend stayed with us and claimed they heard footsteps, too.

Later, after Simone and I had moved, I wondered if the stress in our relationship had reached a pitch so worrisome that someone from the other side came to protect me. I knew it seemed far-fetched, but that night after Simone left, I went to sleep in one of the downstairs bedrooms and when I woke up I realized that I had dreamed of my Aunt Melissa, the one I had called years earlier about my herpes. She had since passed away from lung cancer, at too young of an age. However, when I looked over to the left side of the bed, where I remembered having seen her in my dream, I saw an indentation left by someone sitting there.

Simone and I didn't speak for a few days. Then he called and said he wanted to speak in person. He was crying on the phone. I was reminded of all the times when Tyler convinced me to come back; Simone had the same type of influence on me. He was so upset over the phone and he wanted to talk to me. Thinking it might be the start of a breakthrough moment, I agreed to meet him at a new Hollywood apartment he said he was renting with his business partner.

As soon as I hung up, I asked myself why I had said yes. I was still extremely upset and not looking forward to getting into it with him again. But as always, with my empathetic heart, I figured I would see him and at the very least talk our way through to a more peaceful, understanding place and maybe even get some closure. Then I got to his place and things changed. He was sitting up in his bed and said he wanted to tell me something.

I thought, *Oh no, not again.* What had he been hiding from me all this time? I could feel all my past trauma rising up from behind me like a viper about to strike.

"What?" I asked.

Fighting back tears, he revealed that he was actually years younger than he had initially told me. I think he thought this might make him more sympathetic and his mistakes more understandable and excusable. They didn't. I was stunned. Why hadn't he told me? We had been together about a year, and all along he had been lying to me. Why?

And what was wrong with me that I kept getting myself in these types of situations? Why so much deception? Why was I always finding out something way down the road? Why was it so difficult to get it right?

Then, as if sensing my own weakness, Simone explained that he had been scared to tell me the truth. Scared? I didn't understand. Scared of what? He explained that he feared I might have judged him differently and never accepted him. He was right, of course. If I had known he wasn't in his mid-twenties, as he'd said, but in fact just shy of twenty-one, I would have considered him a fun young man but demurred at getting involved and I wouldn't have been in the situation I was now. But since that wasn't what happened, I didn't know . . .

I didn't know what to do.

I didn't know how to fight for anything.

And I didn't want to fight.

He must have sensed an opening; he kept talking, serving up any reason he could think of to convince me to stay in his life—and I did just that. I was working. I was traveling. I was moving and downsizing. And I persuaded myself, like in so many instances in the past, that things weren't quite as bad as I perceived them and that maybe, hopefully, they would get better. By the end, as happens with so many who've experienced trauma, I was siding with him. If I wasn't perfect, how could I hold others to the same standard?

THE AUGMENT

One problem among the many that went untended: I didn't listen to my instincts. Rather than pay attention to all the inner alarms going off, I told myself that life wasn't perfect and neither were relationships. Which explains why more than a year after that whole scene, Simone and I were engaged, living in my new loft, and planning an Italian wedding for the following summer.

I did everything I could to ensure life was under control and aligned with the fairy-tale images I had in my mind. To that end, I began working out obsessively. Even though Simone had never mentioned any issues with the way I looked, I told myself that I was hitting the gym to keep him happy and embody this idea of what I believed I needed to be. I began lying out in the sun as much as I could, trying to tan. And then I decided to get breast implants. I convinced myself that would make me feel better about myself.

I called my agent and asked for his opinion and help in finding the right doctor to perform the operation. He was my go-to whether I wanted to change my hair color or get a tattoo. I was always concerned about losing work (translation: my appeal) if I changed something about myself. I even told my mother and a few girlfriends.

I wish someone had said something like, "Don't change one damn thing about yourself. It's not natural or healthy. You're perfect. If you aren't happy, change the people around you and the way you live your life. But you are perfect the way you are."

Instead, I was connected to another one of my agent's clients, who had researched the same operation. I was surprised. The actress and I had crossed paths over the years. What is it about beautiful women who get into Hollywood and inevitably begin to think they aren't beautiful enough? Or something-else enough?

In any event, she was wonderful and supportive. I went to her surgeon for a consultation. In the waiting room, I was nervous and on high alert lest anyone recognize me or even seem to. I wanted to keep this a private matter.

The doctor was lovely as we talked in her consultation room. She examined me with sensitivity and we had a matter-of-fact discussion afterward. My breasts were asymmetrical, the right one slightly smaller than the left, which, she said, had more breast tissue. The right one sat a bit higher. Was I aware? Yes, I responded, that was something that I had noticed once many years before and never let go, as if it were proof of my imperfection.

I felt similarly about the size of my breasts. They were little, 32B, and as cliché as it sounded, I admitted I didn't feel womanly enough.

And the antidote? I was given a large binder of porn magazine tear sheets showing women of all breast sizes. The doctor told me to look through the pictures and pick out and notate everything that I liked.

"It will give me the best idea of what you're looking for," she said, and then added, "you can also shape or re-shape the size of your areoles."

"Oh," I said, as if this were a pleasant bonus.

"Whatever you want," she said.

"It's important for me to stay looking natural," I said. "As natural as possible."

"I understand." She stepped back and studied me thoughtfully the way a stylist or photographer might. "I want to bring you up to a full B size, 34B."

"Really?"

"You'll look proportioned," she said.

I relaxed. I was grateful to hear this surgeon identify my problem much the way another doctor might have identified an illness and prescribed a remedy. I had been out of proportion. That was the problem—one of many, but a problem nonetheless. Now that was going to be fixed. I was going to be proportioned. Life would be better.

I had gone through something like this before. When I left Robert, I filled the tiny gaps between my front teeth, a tiny imperfection that people recommended I "do something about." I also addressed my lifelong near-sightedness with laser eye surgery. I cried all morning before that surgery, fearing I would never be the same. I could never wear cool glasses again. Actually, though, my eyesight did improve, and the sentiment behind my tears was correct. I saw these things, the gaps and my eyesight, as flaws, little defects that needed to be corrected in order for me to be better.

But better compared to what?

Closer to perfect according to what model of perfection?

Robert was never a fan of fixing the gaps in my teeth. "They give you character," he said. "They contribute to what makes you you."

However, after I left him, I wanted to feel I was in control of my life and how to live it. I was full of resistance and rebellion and self-loathing. Even though therapy, talk shows, self-help articles, and books had taught me, and indeed convinced me, that self-acceptance, confidence, and whatever else one sought to feel good about themselves had to come from within rather than from plastic surgery, cosmetic procedures, or expensive purchases, I fell victim to the clichés.

I had fixed my teeth, fixed my eyes, and now, four and a half years after leaving Robert and three relationships later, I was fixing my breasts.

The more I looked elsewhere for answers, the further away I got from the only true solution.

"I need to do this," I tried to convincingly tell my girlfriends. "I'll be able to wear dresses and fill in the areas that I never could."

On the morning of my surgery, I recalled a photoshoot I did years earlier for a major women's health and beauty magazine that wanted me on their cover. For the actual cover photos, I wore white jeans with a fitted, bejeweled top. It was a fun look, and I felt pretty. Then, all of a sudden, the mood on the set changed. After the photographer and the magazine's art director huddled in the corner, I was handed a pair of flesh-colored plastic slabs. At first, I was confused. I didn't know what those things were. They had come without explanation. Then I realized they wanted me to put them in my top. They made me huge, much bigger than my authentic body.

"It's the look they're going for," the photographer smiled.

I got it.

And now it made sense. They wanted me *proportioned*.

Simone drove me to the hospital and stayed in the waiting room. Upon my arrival, my plastic surgeon greeted me in her scrubs and marked where the incisions would be made on my chest. Six hours later, the new me came out of the operating room, extremely groggy and extremely swollen. I stayed overnight in the hospital, but I made it through without any complications. I didn't even need painkillers.

The only complication came when I saw myself post-op. Swollen and bandaged, my breasts looked huge, and I freaked. My doctor reassured me the swelling would go down and I would look fine, exactly as we had discussed. My relief was short-lived. I was suddenly terrified that people would know my secret. It was such a perfect example of the contradictions I created for myself. Why have your breasts enhanced if you are scared people will notice? If I was doing it for myself, I shouldn't worry about what others might think or say. I couldn't win because I wouldn't let myself win.

I healed quickly and went off on location to work on a movie, hoping to keep my new shape under wraps. I remained pain-free and no one noticed. The only person on the movie who knew my secret was the one who it bothered—me. I was ashamed and embarrassed of what I had done. I knew better. Every night my head filled with disbelief that I was carrying around plastic bags in my chest.

Was this me?

Had I really done this to myself?

SOMETHING
BORROWED

Simone helped nurse me and my new augmented breasts back to
health, and then it came time for me to decide whether or not
I wanted to move forward with purchasing the loft, because my
lease-to-buy option was coming up. Sigal, who was now back in my life,
advised me against it. It wasn't a good investment, she said matter-of-factly. I
also knew I couldn't afford it.

With her help, Simone and I rented a small house at the end of a cul-de-
sac in the Cahuenga Pass. LA is full of hidden gems like this one—just as it
teems with people guarding secrets, like me post-augmentation—where you
can walk into a little house like ours and something as simple as the expan-
sive view we now had takes your breath away and imbues you with a sense of
hope and possibility as far as you can see.

We got the home for a good price, although still more than the loft per
month, but it was nice to have an entire home with actual doors and separate spaces. We had a couple bedrooms and a large wrap-around patio with
a jacuzzi. I bought a daybed and enjoyed the peace and tranquility and sense
of control I seemed to have when I allowed myself to recline in the sun and
forget about everything.

I was working and made several trips to Toronto, which was convenient
for Simone's contacts. More often than not it felt good to be engaged to
him. But there were a number of times when nothing felt good. I started

to drink, often to excess. I was able to sip white wine when we were in the south of Italy; that lifestyle of sun and vineyards appealed to me. Going to clubs and staying out late with Simone was another story. Too many times I ended the night sick from overindulging in vodka and Redbulls, either over a toilet or doubled over by the side of the road.

Drinking to that degree brought out the worst in me and Simone. In those situations, arguments and tempers escalated as if the alcohol were a truth serum, not only loosening inhibitions but encouraging us to say things we really felt about each other. One night we came home after having some drinks and got into a nasty argument. We were toe-to-toe, screaming at each other out of frustration, desperation, and anger, and the next thing I knew, I hit the floor with a thud. I looked up at Simone, stunned. He seemed equally shaken. We were engaged. This wasn't how it was supposed to go.

But with us, life was a seesaw. It was always back and forth, up and down. The one thing that Simone was extremely good at was convincing me of whatever he sensed I needed to hear. He had a massive talent for talking his way into and out of anything. And I fell for it this time and every other time.

A short while later, we were walking along the street in Toronto when he proposed a business opportunity. As always, I stopped to listen. He started his spiel on the empire he was building and what he needed for the vision to become real. He spoke with the infectious enthusiasm of a gifted sales-man. He needed funds to get things going, he said. He had thought long and hard about how and where to raise the money, and what he proposed doing, what made sense to him, he said, was taking a loan out against my engagement ring.

It was just another moment when I heard the alarms that went off in my head, but I ignored them, wanting instead to believe my life was legit and that I could trust my fiancé.

My eyes fell to my ring. Its ginormous size had always mystified me. I never really knew how Simone had acquired such an expensive item. At the start of our relationship, he introduced me to the jewelers behind this mag-nificent piece. They were friends of his. Once, he had me meet with them about collaborating on a line of jewelry. Nothing came from that meeting, except I was aware of these people in his life.

When Simone finished breaking down how the loan would work, he told me to think about it. I ran the proposition by my entertainment lawyer. She urged me not to do it, explaining that the ring became a gift the moment Simone gave it to me, and that there were certain legal rights surrounding gifts. In short, the ring was mine and I was entitled to keep it if Simone and I ever broke up, which she hoped wouldn't happen, but needed me to be aware of.

She asked how much I thought it was worth. I said about two hundred fifty thousand dollars. She explained that Simone was asking me to legally hand the ring back over to him and I would be relinquishing all rights to it by signing the document he proposed. I understood, but still offered reasons why I was willing to support him. She was kind and patient and repeated her advice to not sign the document, though in the end she said the decision was mine.

"Everything will work out," I told her, feeling slightly embarrassed about what I was implying about our relationship. "Everything will be okay."

I signed the one-page document. I chose to see my decision as one of love and support, and I told Simone the ring itself was unimportant compared to what really mattered in life. If he did well, it would benefit both of us, and that was what I wanted to sparkle more than anything, the two of us and our life together.

There were awkward moments afterward when friends asked why I wasn't wearing my engagement ring. I made up lies. It was being fixed, or refitted, or cleaned prior to our ceremony in Italy. I hated telling lies, especially to friends whose trust in me was automatic and unconditional. When Simone said he was able to get the ring back on loan so I could wear it in our wedding, I didn't know whether to be happy or sick to my stomach that this symbol of our love was now more of a ruse.

Before heading to Italy, Simone and I made our union legal in the US by marrying in a civil ceremony at the Beverly Hills City Hall. I wore a cute sundress, and he cleaned up nicely. Getting to the courtroom was more emotional than I'd anticipated. We parked on a side street and I started crying before I got out of the car. As I opened the door, the tears poured out of me. Simone tried to comfort me.

"We don't have to do this," he said.

Though unable to speak, I shook my head and got out of the car. Once again, I refused to listen to my better instincts, my inner voice, which, like everyone's inner voice, is always the voice of right and reason. And mine was in tears. In fact, my entire body was protesting. But I was having none of it. I ignored all of our fights, the different ways we approached life, and the lies in lieu of locking down my dream wedding in Italy.

I brushed off the rush of emotions as nerves and walked into city hall with Simone. Shortly afterward, we were legally married, husband and wife.

Then it was off to Italy with our nearest and dearest. Simone and I rented a spacious, modern apartment in Rome. On the night before the wedding, he stayed with his family and I slept at the apartment so that we wouldn't see each other again until I walked down the aisle. That night I had the most amazing dream of my life. I was standing in a field of green grass and locked in an embrace with an angel. Both of us were in long, white, flowing gowns. The angel had magnificent, powerful wings. We held hands and began to waltz, and as we did, we lifted off the ground and rose higher and higher and higher into the air and sky. I had never felt such peace and care. I woke up feeling nothing but love.

That day, the last Saturday of June 2010, we gathered at Santo Stefano degli Abissini, an eighth-century private church in Vatican City, for a wedding that was nearly two years in planning and nothing short of spectacular. I felt like a queen in an Alice + Olivia gown that my girlfriend had custom-made, Claudia Cuiti shoes, and Nova diamond earrings. Simone designed our white-gold wedding bands, and the same priest who had married his parents came out of retirement to perform the ceremony. Everything was perfect.

Our reception was at a fifteenth-century castle outside of Rome. During our first dance, an original composition performed by the Gipsy Kings themselves, a gift from two of my best girlfriends, I lost myself in Simone's arms and thought about the dream I'd had the night before, hoping it might be the two of us taking flight together. Everyone was excited to see my engagement ring again and they showered both me and Simone with compliments. None of them knew I was wearing it on loan and it was heading back to Toronto the next day.

So damn embarrassing. I still had no idea what the story was behind it, but I kept eating what he was feeding me and ignoring the fact that bullshit was on the menu.

Sleeplessness

1:30 and I hear each second pass by.

I sit, I wait, I stir, I wonder, I think by myself.

Where do you rest your head when you feel the need?

Does it ever touch a surface you call home?

You remain a mystery to me, unsolvable in every way.

This dark, twelve-hour overcast shadow frightens me.

I feel everything, I hear everything, I see nothing.

This quiet stillness confines me to a multitude of sounds and thoughts.

Does silence ever calm you?

Leave you without the duty of maintaining alertness?

Could I calm you in some way, assume the night shift and keep my guard?

Are all of your nights treated as days?

Have the people you've met and conversed with given warmth to you?

Do you meet the strange, deranged, and unloved?

My wall holds a window that holds a view that holds you wandering somewhere.

My bed comes equipped with three soft, square pillows.

Each occupying a separate space upon the bed.

Seldom dreamt upon, they lie stationed ready for use to end their waiting.

In which direction do you travel?

Would you lay down your weary head?

Could I offer you moments of solitude and peace, instead?

Can I erase the concerns and doubts you feel?

Can I turn off the rude racket of reality?

Can I repair your stability, faith, and knowledge in return for the gifts you once gave me?

Could I hold your hand just one more time?

Yet instead of leading, you'd follow behind.

Any place except the dark we'd visit.

I'd find us a light to start upon the eternal path ahead.

Under umbrellas of toadstools and wet skipping stones, we'd search to uncover our new beginning.

Sure of complete content above all miseries and remaining abundant in cool,

lavish, lush, lazy rests.

Untold of and kept silently secret.

AN AMERICAN HORROR STORY

The day after our glorious ceremony, our broken dynamic returned with the force of a tornado that destroys everything in its path. We were visiting with Simone's family at his nonna's in the city and I noticed that a small stone in my new wedding ring had fallen out. Simone flipped out. He did it in front of his whole family, criticizing me for not noticing the missing stone until now. His anger was unrelenting and left me mortified.

He continued to berate me back in our apartment. He didn't stop all day, which turned what was supposed to be our romantic getaway into a nightmare. That night, with his anger still out of control, I reached a point where I feared for my safety and ran into the bedroom, locking the door behind me. Simone tried to get in and the door gave way. Seeing the way he looked at me frightened me even more, and I knew I had to get out of there. I packed my things and his cousin came and got me.

Outside, I sat in his cousin's car, crying and uncertain of what to do. I felt like I was losing my mind. His cousin tried to console me, but he didn't speak English and I didn't speak Italian and it just felt extremely awkward. I was embarrassed for seeming hysterical and out of control without being able to explain why.

How could I go back to Simone?

How could I have gone back to Tyler all those times?

It's what I knew. Here I was in Rome, sitting in a car with all my things in the trunk, and it was the same as when I used to drive around Los Angeles with all my belongings in the back of my car, swearing I wasn't going back to Tyler. Yet all I ever did was go back.

This time was no different. We returned to LA, where our landlord informed us that he wanted to take over our house, so we had to find a new home. It should have seemed like a blessing, a sign that we could begin our marriage with a blank canvas, and that was the way it looked on the surface. With help from Sigal, we found a beautiful house near the reservoir in the Cahuenga Pass. With lots of natural elements incorporated in its design, the place had a magical, Zen-like quality. Simone fell in love with the large saltwater pool in the backyard. It was paradise, except for the cost. This place was significantly more expensive than our previous rental, and I didn't feel like Simone was contributing enough toward the expenses.

Besides our home and our recent wedding, the bills I paid also included the lease on his BMW. To cover everything, I was having to dip into my pension.

Simone seemed to work longer hours as he focused even more on building his company. He started to call himself a manager instead of a promoter. Whenever I asked where he was going, he answered the studio. He was always in the studio. I enjoyed the additional time I had to myself. These moments were peaceful. They gave me time to think with a clarity that was impossible when we fought and I was upset. But with all the time Simone spent in the studio, sometimes all night, I began to feel like we were spending more time apart than together.

Then he left town to work in Canada. This was shortly after we had moved into the house. We were still living amid unpacked boxes, but I wished him well and said I would take care of settling us in. I wanted to be supportive. While he was out of town, I booked a job on the anthology series *American Horror Story*, one of my favorite shows. I was playing the ghost of the Black Dahlia, who returns to haunt a murder house unaware that she's dead. I had been working very hard to keep everything going, and it felt like a personal win for me to get this particular part. It was an excellent role and a dream opportunity to work with the show's stellar cast.

The work started while Simone was away in Canada, but I still had a couple days of shooting left when he returned, and I was excited to be able to share time with him and have his support. Though I had to be at work early the morning after he came back, I still had hopes of lingering in bed with Simone. But when I woke up, I was surprised to find that he was already up and getting ready to leave the house. He said he was meeting a buddy at the gym.

Surprised and hurt, I wished we could have had time together but I didn't want to have an argument. Instead I invited him to come by the set later and visit if he had time. We kept in touch throughout the day and I arranged for him to come by during our lunch break. I got him a visitor's pass so he could park near our dressing room trailers on the studio lot.

I was rarely comfortable having visitors on a set, and this time even more so. As a guest star, I was aware that I was coming into a place where people had established their ways and I didn't want to disturb anyone's routine. And on top of all that, I never felt I was good enough. I knew how to do my job but always pushed myself to do it better, especially on this set, which taxed me further. But I was looking forward to enjoying my break with Simone.

Our lunch break was actually around dinnertime, and I ate beforehand in order to have more free time. Then Simone showed up, and suddenly I wanted to crawl down some damn hole and die. I was being driven in a golf cart to the set from the dressing room trailers when I heard the loud *vroooooommmmmm* of a sports car revving its engine. I wondered what asshole was doing that on the lot, where every soundstage and building had a sign reminding people to be quiet, which was especially needed when red lights flashed outside their doors. That's when I saw my husband, heading toward me, in the passenger seat of a red convertible Lamborghini being driven by one of his friends.

I flagged them down and told them where to park, hoping that not too many people saw. But I felt like the damage had been done. I was deeply embarrassed. By the time Simone and his friend met me on the set, I was managing to hide my feelings about the way they had paraded around the lot in that car. I tried introducing Simone to one of the producer-writers.

That was also a disaster. Simone and his friend were too busy grazing at the craft service table full of food and snacks. He behaved more like a five-year-old than my husband.

I was crushed. Being on this show was such a big opportunity for me, and I hoped and prayed that no one would look at me in a different light because of Simone's behavior. I just wanted to do my job and be as respectful of the space as possible, and here he rolls up like he's inspecting his empire. I plastered a fake smile on my face until he left; finally, Simone said he was going out to dinner with his friend, which I said was fine with me because I probably wouldn't be done filming until midnight.

By this point, it was close to ten and I was curious how late he planned to be out, because I didn't want to worry. Sometimes he would be in the studio all night. We also still hadn't spent any time together for more than two weeks. He assured me that he wouldn't be late and would see me at home. We said goodbye, and I went back to the set not knowing that this would be the last night of our relationship.

When I arrived home a little after midnight, Simone wasn't there. I was disappointed but too tired to think about it. I had my own full life and didn't want to hold him back from pursuing the same thing. I got into bed and went to sleep. I woke up around five, hoping to find him next to me. But he still wasn't home. Since he had pointedly said he wasn't going to be out late, I panicked. I imagined him in the hospital. Or dead someplace without anyone knowing. I didn't have any messages on my phone, which compounded my fears. I tried calling him, without getting an answer. I did this two, three, four, then six times. Each time, the call rang and went to voicemail. I hung up and redialed.

I was worried and angry and ultimately so sick of having drama in my life. Why were all my relationships fraught with such intense issues? I wanted to scream.

An hour passed and I still couldn't reach him. The sun was starting to come up. I was out of my mind with what to do next. Exhausted, I wished I could have stayed asleep or could go back to sleep, but it was impossible for me to lay my head back down on my pillow and act as if nothing were wrong. I didn't know his friend personally, so I had no other numbers to call. All I could do was sit in bed and wait, which felt excruciating. Finally, after what seemed like hours, I heard the garage door open. I leapt out of bed and ran into the hallway, eager to know where he had been.

I was waiting when he entered the main house and barely able to get out "Where were you?" before he blew past me and went into the half bath off the living room, shutting the door without stopping to even acknowledge me. Now, not only was I irritated, I was becoming enraged. The door to the half bath was frosted, so I could see his figure sitting on top of the toilet. He wasn't using it; he was just sitting there. I tried the door. It was locked.

"Open the door," I said.

He mumbled something I couldn't make out.

"Open the door," I said again.

He ignored me and sat there a little bit longer before getting up and coming out. By this point, I was so damn confused, angry, and exhausted that I had walked back into the bedroom, where I sat up in the bed. Desperate to stay calm, I was poised and statue-like as I waited for him. When he finally entered the room, he continued to ignore me and walked around to his side of the bed.

"Where were you?" I asked again.

Wordlessly, Simone took off his clothes, like he was going to get into bed, as if everything were normal, as if it were normal to have not answered his phone all night, as if it were normal to come home at six in the morning without any explanation and nonchalantly lie down while I repeatedly implored him to talk to me. For a second or two, I thought he was going to say that he had cheated on me.

I prepared myself to deal with that news. Once again, I asked him where he had been, and as he pulled back the covers to lay his head down, he finally confessed what he had been up to.

Hearing that made everything stop. I had been looking at Simone, but my gaze changed so that I was trying to see inside him. I thought about what he was telling me and what he was not telling me.

His actions and admission left me to form my own opinion about what he was saying, and if it was true, I was done. I wanted nothing to do with him.

He had lied to me about his age. Suddenly, I had no idea if he'd always been in the studio or if that was code for something else he was doing and hiding. And now this admission. I couldn't believe it, but after five years together, it dawned on me that I had no idea who this person lying next to me in bed really was; before his head hit the pillow, I said, "Get the fuck out of here."

"I'LL FIND A WAY!"

walked into the living room and grabbed Simone's keys. I wanted him to leave, and I needed a safe space for myself. I had prided myself for being in control of my life, and the reality couldn't have been more different. It was an absolute fucking disaster. The evidence was right in front of me. Right next to me, in fact. But not for long.

Simone went into the garage. I wondered if he was going to take my car, a 600 class Benz that he had convinced me to buy for ninety thousand dollars. Years later, after I had taken over my own accounting, I learned that I could have leased it and written off approximately seventy percent. I also realized that I could no more afford that car than I could a private jet. Simone and I were living in an even more opulent house than before, and I had signed a two-year lease. But booking *American Horror Story* had given me the sense that more opportunity was up ahead. I had tried so hard to create something with Simone, but it wasn't manifesting and I knew why. I hadn't listened to my heart when I walked into that courtroom that day and married him; my soul had burst out crying. Now, as I watched him walk around the backyard in a comedown haze, I didn't shed a single tear. Instead I felt relief.

I continued to watch Simone through the glass bedroom doors. It was a beautiful ranch-style home, and the side of the house that faced the backyard was pretty much glass; it was gorgeous. Simone had come around to the backyard and was pleading with me to let him in. He was upset about the coyotes in the backyard, which were a figment of his delusional imagination.

Compassion and capitulation were always my go-tos, but I wanted to flip the script here. I was pissed. I was done living this life. How dare he stay out all night, come home early in the morning, and walk into the bedroom like he was going to sleep without any explanation? Was I supposed to accept that because we were married?

Way down in my gut I was always suspicious, but never did anything about it. However, as I'd heard people say, the Universe is always trying to communicate with us, and when we still aren't listening, it will, one way or another, make the lesson so apparent that you have no choice but to pay attention. Well, the Universe had my attention. Working on *American Horror Story* had given me a glimpse into what more could come of my life by believing in myself. I supposed that had always been the issue. I had never believed in myself enough to fight back, to say no, to say no more, no fucking way.

I packed Simone's clothes while he continued to walk around outside. I went into the kitchen; he watched me from outside the window. I called his mother and told her that it would probably be in Simone's best interests if she called him. I sensed he needed to hear from her, I explained. After I hung up, Simone was standing near me, mortified. He couldn't believe that I had called his mother. But you know what? He needed help. It just wasn't going to come from me anymore.

After a while, Simone left. He took the suitcase I packed with some of his clothes. I gathered the rest for him to take another time. The house was quiet and still. I walked over to the side of my bed and sat down on the platform. I must have been in shock; I couldn't believe my marriage was over and I was going to have to go through another divorce. And this house. How was I going to afford this house? What was I going to do?

I felt overwhelmed, like giant weights had settled on my shoulders and were pushing me down. But then, suddenly and out of nowhere, I just stopped. I stopped everything and I said out loud to the Universe, "Bring it. 'Cause I don't care anymore. I'll find a way. Throw whatever you want at me, I'll figure it out. I will figure it out!"

At that moment, I felt invigorated, energized, and something I hadn't felt in as long as I could remember. I felt strong. I suppose I was always strong without knowing it, but now I knew it. I wasn't going to allow the fear to enter my thoughts, my life, my being. I would find another way. I didn't need anyone in my life. I might choose to have someone in it, but I didn't *need* someone.

I had no idea what my next steps would be. But I felt such faith that I would make it through.

That faith was tested as soon as I initiated divorce proceedings. I found a lawyer willing to handle both Simone and me for a set fee, which was economical and efficient, as we really had nothing to dispute. But Simone decided to get his own attorney. This put me in a difficult financial position. Because I was considered the breadwinner, I had to pay all costs. Since he knew as well as I did the limit of my assets, I felt like he did that purposely to make me suffer. His demands included the use of my car for six months and seventeen thousand dollars a month in support, a ridiculous amount that, again, I thought was meant only to antagonize me. I had no interest in engaging in a fight. I wanted to cut ties and move on with my life as quickly and smoothly as possible. No more games. No more nonsense. I spoke to Sigal, who helped get me out of the two-year lease I had signed, and I began to channel my energy into mending my life.

And that's when I met Sal.

No More

If I had decided to give up last night
The desk I now occupy would be empty
And the attire I present would not be worn
But the headache in my brain would be no more.

If I threw up my hands and prayed to go
The strangers around me would never know
The hall and the streets would hear me no more
While my possessions collected oldness and dust from lying
alone.

Had I committed the act the house would fall silent
Soothing vocals of Perry would never be heard
The sweet Nag Champa would burn no more
And the breeze from outside would fly through my room.

If I decided to leave to escape from this place
Who knows where I'd go or what I would see
My home would fall empty, my bed would turn cold
And those words that I've collected would never have been told.

"SWEET SOUL SAL"

Years earlier, I'd gotten my first tattoo. As an actress, I'd been worried that I needed to be a blank canvas. And personally, I hadn't seen getting any part of my body permanently inked. But one day, after beginning to make the connection between my past as a survivor and the new path I wanted for myself, I knew I wanted one. But not just any tattoo. I knew exactly what I wanted—and where on my body I wanted it.

Finding the right person to do it took time. Through friends, I was introduced to Mister Cartoon, a Los Angeles legend whose reputation was worldwide. Once I saw his artwork, I knew he was the right person for me. I went to his studio in downtown LA.

"I want a lion's head on the back of my neck," I told him, explaining how the spirituality of animals resonated with me and I wanted to keep that energy around me. "The lion represents strength and courage. I had a vision of it on the back of my neck as protection from whatever might try to attack me spiritually from behind."

He was a good listener. After taking it all in, he pulled an image he already had of a lion head and gave it to me to inspect.

"I love it," I said. "I can't believe it. This is exactly what I wanted and never could have been able to articulate. It's so . . . powerful . . . and strong. It's perfect."

It was also beautiful—a beautiful piece of artwork done in black and grey. The whole experience of meeting him and picking out the image was easy, as if it were meant to be. I sensed the Universe supporting me.

Cartoon's assistant started to prepare the station for my tattoo. He was a sweet young guy who told me his name was Sal. I wondered if he knew how intimidated I was to be in the studio, me being a white girl in this place steeped in the culture of East LA Latinos and South Central LA Blacks. It turned out he did. But he also picked up on the fact that I was there not because I was trying to be hip or doing something radically chic but because I was drawn by Cartoon's mastery and the power of his work, and that opened the door to a more personal conversation.

That and music. Right away we discovered a mutual love for particular songs and musicians, and after my tattoo was done we kept in touch sporadically until the calls stopped and email addresses changed. Years later, he mentioned that his emails had bounced back and at one point, feeling like he wanted to talk, he'd reached out but never heard back. Our lives diverged. I would go on to meet Simone and get married.

After Simone and I separated, though, I wanted to add a few more tattoos. I felt a new sense of freedom and empowerment and I wanted that reflected on my body. I wanted to feel it and see it. Shortly after getting my lion, I had traveled to Africa for the African Medical Research Foundation, or AMREF. We went into remote areas of Uganda and Ethiopia, where I sat in on a cleft palate surgery for a one-year-old baby, met with AIDS activists, and visited with women who were given the tools to get them off the streets and start their own businesses. During a welcoming ceremony in Ethiopia, I was given the name Selam, which means "peace."

Almost five years after that trip I walked back into Mister Cartoon's studio, wanting to capture that clear, pure, and strong sense of self and being I remembered from Africa. And in that moment, Sal came back into my life. This time we didn't let each other get away. After making sure we had the right contacts, Sal began sending me songs with cryptic messages embedded in the accompanying notes. I loved his taste and the sensitivity he shared in explaining his choices.

Soon we were texting each other messages of affection. Many days, he simply texted, "Have a beautiful day." Or, remembering that I had a meeting or audition, he wished me luck. I felt like I had sunshine on my face. He was so kind, and that was something unusual for me to deal with. It almost made me uncomfortable, that's how much I didn't know how to accept someone simply being nice to me.

He was breaking up with his girlfriend and I was obviously on my own again. Very quickly our texting turned into talking and that led to an understanding that we were going to take our friendship to the next level. We met up one night after he finished work, and when I arrived, as he closed up shop, he asked me if I wanted to take a cruise. His '88 Monte Carlo shimmered in the moonlight. Excited to spend time with him, I climbed into his car and we drove over the Sixth Street Bridge and into his East LA neighborhood. It felt like we were leaving reality, the only car on the road, indeed the only two people driving around in the city—a city of angels.

I made sure we addressed the serious stuff happening in his relationship, and once I was satisfied that I wasn't playing a role in a breakup, which I made clear he needed to deal with before we could move forward, I sat back and enjoyed the feeling of my heart filling with happiness. Sal circled back toward downtown and parked in front of the Urth Caffé in the Arts District. Earlier on our drive, our forearms had very softly touched and it sent shivers up and down my spine. Now I was feeling them again.

He hurried around his car and opened my door. He was such an old-school gentleman, the reason he became known as my "Sweet Soul Sal." I had never been treated this way, and it was wonderful to be out with someone who wanted to make sure I was cared for and felt happy. We walked up to the Urth Caffé and got in line. Though it was after ten, the place was crowded and lively. The wait was twenty to thirty minutes. I didn't mind. I was content to wait and talk with Sal.

Time passed quickly and we were thinking about what we wanted to order when my phone rang. I saw it was my brother and told Sal I needed to take it. At this hour, I knew it couldn't be good news—and it wasn't.

PAPA

Excusing myself, I told Sal that I needed to take the call and walked out to the street to get some space and privacy. I said hello and heard my brother crying as he started to talk. Reflexively, I crossed the street and tucked myself in the doorway of an industrial building on the corner. In the dark, hidden from light and shadows, I heard my brother say, "Papa just died."

I had thought about this day—no, this moment—for ages and yet I still wasn't prepared for the impact it had on me. My father had been sick since I was a teenager. After having his first mild stroke, his mind had slowly deteriorated. As a psychiatrist, he had helped so many people over decades. He worked for the state of Rhode Island for twenty-five years. He had been early to embrace holistic and herbal treatments rather than chemical pharmaceuticals, if and when appropriate. He was on the forefront, but he lost a lot of that present and purposeful state of mind as he aged. That was always the hardest thing for me to experience.

I was born late in his life and never got to experience the best or sharpest of his years. It was one of my great regrets and for years I wondered how my life might have been different if I could have had his insight and counsel. I also felt guilty that care for him late in life had fallen on my brother's shoulders.

My heart broke as I listened to my brother cry. I realized that I had never heard him cry or bare his emotions. He had always been so resilient, so happy-go-lucky all the time. But here he was trying to tell me what had happened, and he was unable to get the words out. I wished I could have been there and done more, but I kept that to myself and was later glad I did, because the truth was, I could have done more but I didn't.

"Did he pass easily?" I asked.

It was hard for my brother to explain our father's last moments. And it felt even harder to hear.

After hanging up, I was in a state of shock and sadness. I wondered if my father knew that I loved him. I think he knew I loved him. I visited him so many times over the years. He was living in a care facility, and each time I saw him, I thought it might be the last time. One time in particular, after seeing him so sick and feeble and out of it, I collapsed in the facility's stairwell. I just couldn't bear seeing him like that. It was soul crushing to sit by his side, talk to him, hold his hand, and know he didn't know who I was anymore. I was his daughter and he didn't know me. My father had always been much older than anyone else's father. He was around sixty years old when I was born. I had beautiful and fun memories of being with him when I was young, but we had lost the connection by the time that I needed him most. By the time that I was a teenager and so desperately lost, my family had fallen apart and splintered. I was only in my midteens when he had his first stroke, and it destroyed me. It drove me away from him, away from home, and added so much to the problems I had growing up.

I stood in the dark, hidden from the world, perfectly still, staring blankly at the outdoor diners across the street and listening to myself breathe. I had no idea what to do with myself. I was overcome by the news and what this meant to me and my family. At the same time I felt badly that I had left Sal in line, waiting for me, without knowing what was really going on. I felt devastated and completely lost until I walked back across the street and let Sal in on the news. He provided the anchor of sanity I needed.

"Let's go over to my car and talk," he said, placing his hand on my shoulder and gently guiding me away from the restaurant.

The poor guy. We were just getting to know each other and suddenly I was dealing with my father's death on our first date. But with such grace, he created space that allowed me to feel safe enough to cry and be within myself until I exhausted my tears. Finally, I looked up at him with an apologetic shake of my head.

"Let me get some food to go," he said. "You haven't eaten and neither have I. It's not going to help either one of us if we're hungry."

He opened up his driver's side door and, after glancing back my way, he headed across the street toward the café. When he got back, Sal drove us someplace quiet and I opened up about my dad in a way I hadn't to anyone else.

"There was always such a deep, dark hole, an abyss, where I felt like my father should have been—or where I wish he would have been. And it just grew. I'm glad my father won't have to suffer anymore. I hope his soul passed peacefully."

It was a lot to share with someone, especially someone I hardly knew, but Sal was remarkable. He stayed present with me, listening as we ate and talked—or rather, as I talked—and the night ended with me feeling like he had been a precious gift to me, a light when I could have so easily been enveloped by a forever-type of darkness.

By the time he walked me to my car in the parking lot near Cartoon's studio and we said goodnight, he was a good friend, someone who, no matter where our new relationship went, would, for the time and sensitivity he gave me that night, be forever imprinted on my heart.

In the days afterward, Sal and I texted and tried to get together, but time did not work in our favor. Saying goodbye to my father took a week and then I had to travel to Australia for a junket and the premiere of *American Pie: Reunion*. I texted Sal from the airport, saying I was aware of his situation in the same way he was aware of mine and I wanted to keep in touch when and if it worked.

He wrote back that he was committed to taking care of his situation and that he hoped to continue to get to know me more. I read and reread that note, and with love in my heart again, I set off for Australia, feeling completely grateful to have such an honest and gentle soul come into my life.

JUSTICE

A unique thing happened with Sal. Because I had to travel right after our first date, I wasn't able to sabotage the relationship. Every time I had entered a relationship, or even had any kind of attraction toward someone, I rushed into an intimacy before getting to know the person and learning whether the situation was even right. But having to be away from Sal turned out to be something so beautiful and powerful because we couldn't be together right away and had to get to know each other. We had to talk.

And we talked. On the phone and over FaceTime. For hours. I had much more free time than he did, but the time difference between Sydney and Los Angeles worked in our favor. The wee hours of the night in LA when he was finishing up at the studio were still early evening in Australia, just a day apart. Every day I was there was brightened by looking forward to the next moment we would speak.

When I returned to Los Angeles we were a full-fledged couple. I couldn't see my life without this sensitive soul, and I didn't want to. He opened my eyes to ways the world worked and showed me a new way of understanding life beyond the privilege of what I was used to. He had such a clear sense of right and wrong and just and unjust.

Divorcing Simone was costing me a fortune. He hadn't needed to get his own representation, as the lawyer I found was ready to handle our pretty easy case, but just to spite me, he put me in a position where I had to pay his lawyer's and immigration fees. I remember complaining to Sal that it wasn't right. He explained what was right didn't always jibe with what was the law. "I get it," I said. "I've been taken advantage of, manipulated, or used my whole life. I'm done. I want to fight for what's right."

"You have to," he said.

Ironically, the first person I fought with afterward was Sal. Together for about six months by this time, we returned from dinner with some friends one night and something happened, a small thing, the details of which have faded. I remember it as a minor misunderstanding, but it triggered me into feeling like Sal was disrespecting me. He wasn't, of course. It was because of my always-ever-looming trauma mixed with being so on edge from the divorce entanglements and financial pressures grinding on me that I took it out on Sal, the one person who was kind, patient, and loving toward me.

It was as if I needed to sabotage our relationship because it was too good and I had to prove to myself that it was impossible to love me. But he wouldn't let me. Though it was late, we walked up to the dog park near the Hollywood Sign and sat down on some rocks. I closed my eyes and heard him take a deep breath and exhale. When I opened my eyes again, he was looking at me with a disarming openness. He had no anger, no judgment, no tension in him, whereas I was tightly wound and ready to snap again.

"Talk to me," he said.

I wanted to fight, but when I looked in his eyes I saw nothing but care and concern, and it led me to try something different: talk. After taking a few minutes to calm myself, I told him what was bothering me, really bothering me—not the bit I had accused him of back home, but the frustration, insecurity, and pressure I was battling as a result of my screwed-up life, for seeming to not be able to escape it, and the anger I had toward everyone, especially myself.

"I can't seem to get out of the shit," I said. "I work so hard to be good and healthy and loving and a light, and still everything is fucked-up."

Sal and I sat for hours, talking and talking until I was talked out. I stared up at the moon as it crept across the night sky. Only as I wearied did I notice the air had turned chilly. Sal was present, accepting, considerate, and loving the whole time. I was sure half the things I said were impossible to understand. My sentences were clipped and my thoughts coded in a shorthand that referenced a past about which he knew very little. Navigating through the pain was a struggle for me. So much was stuff I had never articulated.

I didn't have the words. Sal sat beside me patiently, his silence and strength encouraging me to find the words and comforting me afterward.

He was more than just an emotional support. I went to Vancouver for work, and while there I realized Simone was supposed to return my car, the S600 Mercedes-Benz. Through our attorneys, I'd agreed to his controlling ask to let him use the car for six months before returning it in the same pristine condition I kept it. If he wanted it longer, he had to submit a written request at least fourteen days in advance. While I was in Vancouver, I realized Simone's six months were ending the next day and I proceeded to take steps to make sure he returned it.

I needed to get rid of that car; I couldn't afford it anymore. I called Simone, who said he couldn't give the car back because he was going to be out of town.

"Then how about dropping it off today?" I said.

"That won't work," he said. "I was hoping you would understand."

I didn't. I was livid. As I had told Sal long before, I was sick of always having to navigate through someone else's bullshit games. I insisted he get it back to me, one way or another. We had an agreement and time had run out.

But he wouldn't budge. He simply didn't care and loved to throw it in my face that I wouldn't be able to do anything. Or so he thought.

"Well, I'm going to call the police and report the car as stolen, then," I said.

"Don't threaten me with the fucking cops!" he erupted. "I don't care about the fucking cops!"

I was shaking when I hung up the phone. I stared at my trembling hands and decided to turn this sense of violation and weakness into strength. *No more*, I told myself. I booted up my computer and researched which department at the LAPD dealt with stolen cars. I found a number for a detective and called. It went straight to voicemail. I left a message but never heard back. I knew my car was part of Simone's whole look and he couldn't afford to not have it as validation of the impression he wanted to make. I called Sal and asked for advice on getting someone from LAPD to call back. He cut me off midway through the story.

"I'm here," he said. "I'm getting your car."

No time had been wasted. During my time trying to locate an officer to report the issue to, Sal and a friend of his—a big scary-looking dude covered in tattoos, but with his heart in the right place—showed up at Simone's place and got the car. According to what he told me afterward, it seemed like they got there just in time. Simone was packing his things into another car, like he was about to head out of town, as he'd said, and it appeared my car was going to sit in his driveway.

Then Sal said something that just made me feel horrible. He told me how he and his friend saw Simone acting; it seemed as if nothing had changed. I felt shocked and sad.

"It's over," Sal said. "You can move on."

"Thank you. Thank you, Sal."

I opened the curtains in my hotel room and looked out the window. Vancouver was lovely, colorful, fresh.

He was right. I always gave so much of myself. I simply wanted to be happy. I still did. Now I had the opportunity to try for something new in my life.

STARTING FRESH

I was still living in the house in Lake Hollywood but desperate to get out. I couldn't afford it. Every morning, Sal and I drove to a different neighborhood, where we had breakfast and walked around, loving the area for its bohemian vibe and creative energy. It was alive. We felt good there, like we belonged. We kept talking about how we wished we could live there. It was clear I had to try to get out of my expensive lease.

I spent weeks composing a letter to my landlord. Sigal worked on it with me and read it numerous times. I obsessed over every fact and word and the overall tone. It felt embarrassing and irresponsible to have to be doing this.

Finally, I sent the letter and tried not to think about it, though of course I thought of nothing else. My landlord had every right to hold me to the lease, but he emailed a day or two later, saying he understood my situation and wished me luck. Better for him to have someone who could send in rent rather than excuses, and as mortified as I was about having to admit my dire straits, I was relieved. I had never taken responsibility for my finances, and so, clearly, the time had come. I had feared people knowing that I was struggling and opening myself up to ridicule and not feeling in control. All of those things.

I was starting fresh. The Universe was opening a door for me. Something was guiding me and I needed to go with it. Within a week of getting word that I could break my lease, a rental opportunity came up in the neighborhood where Sal and I wanted to live. Even better, the cute little property was one we had specifically eyed as a fantasy home if it were ever to be available, and now it was. We took it.

We moved into our new home and settled in. Living together felt right and made me happy. On the surface, we looked like polar opposites. I was white, blonde, and Hollywood. He was brown, his hair slicked back in old-school Chicano style, and East LA. Photographs of us surfaced. The way we were judged and misunderstood only made us feel prouder of the way we loved each other. People always failed to see the similarity of human hearts.

From the first time we were together, we worked very hard to stay present and discuss every issue. I had never been in a loving, supportive, caring relationship. We enjoyed leisurely breakfasts, long walks, and making each other laugh. We were kind and considerate and patient with each other, and we pursued deep, challenging, emotional, and therapeutic conversations that lasted late into the night. Disagreements were rare, but when we did have a dispute, one of us usually broke the tension by bursting into laughter. We hated to argue with each other.

Two years into our relationship, the night that we had sat beneath the Hollywood sign and talked for hours remained an inspiring touchstone. That night, I had tried to explain what I was looking for at this point in my life. I felt like I had devised a pretty good dynamic of what that would look like and I had worked hard to finally express it. Sal had heard me and taken all necessary measures to incorporate that into our lives. And here I was in a relationship where both of us led with love.

My career was up and down. I had blown more money than I would ever know. But when I needed someone to listen to me, hold me, or support me, Sal's arms were always wide-open and waiting for me. For the first time, my life was easy. I wanted to begin again. I wanted to move past the trauma of the past and heal.

I knew I had felt that way before.

This time, though, something was different.

I didn't know how I was going to do it and I knew it wasn't going to be easy. But I was finally ready.

Really ready.

CREATING SPACE

Throughout our relationship, I had a series of emotional breakdowns. I was always trying to stay as active as possible in my healing, and I did take good care of myself physically. But I overlooked myself emotionally. The breakdowns came suddenly and without warning, as if the floor just opened up and swallowed me whole. My mind fell into the darkest place imaginable without there seeming to be any way out. Every single bit of fear and shame that I had felt over the years was forever on simmer.

With Sal, I saw that I had someone in my life who I trusted to help me finally overcome some of these emotional obstacles and hopefully put an end to these spells when I fell apart. One day, while we were relaxing at home, I knew what I needed to do. I had been feeling heavily emotional since the morning, and I couldn't stop thinking about what I needed to do for myself, which was to talk. I needed to stop, take a deep breath, let the emotions I felt in my heart connect with my brain, and put them into words. I needed to speak.

I needed to get all that shit I had been carrying around out of me.

I had never told anyone everything, and I was still scared to speak up. I didn't know if I could hold up while revealing such foulness. I had suffered badly after telling Jay that I was infected with herpes. So revealing everything? It was like my whole life was one horrendous infection. However, something told me that the only way I could hope to heal was to speak up for myself, to speak out . . . out, out, out. It was like an exorcism.

I was damned if I did and damned if I didn't. The most painful of Catch-22s. But, ultimately, I saw that I had only one choice—and I chose me.

I told Sal that I wanted to talk to him, which he was instantly amenable to, but I added that I needed him to sit across the room from me. In a chair. And with his back to me. All the instructions surprised him, and I think they might have also made him sad, as he wished he could be more accessible to me during what was clearly something very important.

He walked over to the chair, sat down, and swiveled it around to face the back window looking out toward the Hollywood Hills. I stepped over to the shag rug and sat down cross-legged. Right away I felt my throat close up. Blockage. It was very easy for me to think of my trauma, especially to visualize it. The images appeared in my head with high-definition resolution. An album depicting the worst moments of my life. Fragments frozen in time. The most helpless and painful moments. I had been a victim for too long. I wanted a new role.

I shut my eyes and took deep breaths, and when I opened them again, I started to summon the words. Within seconds, I was hyperventilating. Every word I said put me right back into the moment, into the cycle of trauma that I wanted to escape. I had jumped back into the riptide and felt myself being pulled back out to sea. I flailed in the depths of shame and hurt. The pressure on my chest was almost unbearable. I tried to focus and stay on track. I needed to get rid of all this darkness in order to create space for healing light.

I went back to the beginning. I described meeting Tyler. I told him the different ways I thought he sexually abused me, the ways that abuse manifested and morphed into more, along with the verbal humiliation. I shared all the details of my circumstances, the way we had lived, the things I felt like I had been coerced into doing, the things I was forced to accept, and all the frustration and shame of keeping that hidden.

I didn't think I could say any of this, and then I didn't think I could stop. There was so much anger in my voice. I had felt such intense anger, resentment, and bitterness over what had happened to me. I was pissed that no one had rescued me. I was pissed at myself for feeling so weak and worthless. And I was pissed at the Universe for throwing what I felt was way too much at me to handle.

Sal had a very difficult time sitting in the chair. He desperately wanted to get up and run over to hold me so that I would feel loved and supported. He wanted me to know that I could feel safe. But I stopped him. I needed him to give me space and simply be there. Just hold the space and listen. I needed someone to listen. That's what had been missing: someone to listen to me. The words were so hard to find. They swirled in my head, debris caught up in a funnel cloud. I would see an image, feel the pain in my soul, find myself thrust right back in the moment, but then suddenly I was released.

I had to keep going through each one.

I told Sal of the big-breasted girl. I told him of the other girls Tyler called up and invited to be with us. I told him how I had never wanted any of those things. How I had felt trapped and bound and helpless to leave. I told him how I didn't think I had any other place to go. How I numbed myself each day in order to not feel what was happening with my body. How no matter how much pot I smoked, I still felt everything. How I had felt trapped forever because of the herpes. How I convinced myself the loving thing to do was accept that condition. How I also accepted Tyler giving me crabs . . .

How I would forever feel ashamed by allowing my body to be disrespected by the sex toys being used on me. How I was taken, time after time, to find what the next sex toy could be; how big a dildo he could buy to make me use. How, one day, he brought a double-headed dildo into one of his sex-capades, so he could watch me "fuck" another girl. How he would become wild to fuck me quick for a few seconds, just so he could fuck the other girl for what felt like forever while I lay there watching, unsure of what to do, but being encouraged by him to continuously engage. Feeling so high, from numbing my brain from the pain, so that I didn't even care what my body was doing. How I just, so easily, destroyed any part of what I considered the right thing to be taking place; I had relented so fully and completely that I created my own objectification. How I just couldn't see around me any of the opportunity or beauty that was also possible. How the pain and guilt I felt over not fighting back more was heavier than I would have imagined. And how while I hated going along with his sexual escapades, I was not emotionally equipped to say no. It's possible he even had no idea of the damage he'd done to me. Years after finally freeing myself of him, I had run into him on the street, and he acted surprised and denied how abusive and destructive our relationship ever was. How that became the final abuse of his that kept the bindings of my trauma tight, because he couldn't even, ever, admit to it. I would be the one left with having to come to terms with it. I would be the one left with facing my abuse every single time I became too stressed from it, because I would get an outbreak. I had to live with this virus that he had given me. I would be the one forever living with the physical manifestation of his lack of respect and responsibility. Every moment forward, every relationship of mine . . . I was bound back to him. Every single step of the way where I should have, organically, had the chance to discover myself. Even discover my womanhood or myself sexually, but that was robbed from me. The only option I ever had was to relent to what was around me. I had become aware of how this abuse had created a rift inside me; I wasn't able to create my own opinion of something based upon my own desire to do so, or gain the knowledge that would have come with creating it. Tyler had already decided those things for me. And I had allowed it, because I had no strength to fight it. I was severely humiliated, but then when fame came, I simply stored it all away, as if it were never a part of my history, because I didn't know how to incorporate it. And if anything, I relished in any opportunity to feel as if those things had never even happened to me; I preferred to acknowledge the part of "myself" that everyone only loved and adored. But now, with Sal, it was time for me to take responsibility for what I was going to do with that pain. I couldn't fight it anymore, and I was tired of suffering from it, too. I continued to sob, even heave uncontrollably, as each word came out of my mouth. Hearing it caused the pain to become even worse, but I powered through. No matter how much more pain there was to come, my desire to rid myself of it helped carry me forward.

By the time I finished, it felt like we had spent a lifetime together. I suppose we had. Both of us were crying when we finally faced each other. I knew how hard it had been on Sal, but I thanked him and said the most important thing was that he was still there. He had given me space, he had listened, and he had done it without any judgment. He had made me feel safe. And for the first time in my life, I felt relief.

I couldn't believe I had actually voiced everything. I couldn't believe I was still there and in one piece after doing so.

Whether Tyler, KJ, or Iain ever agreed with me was not my problem or an issue that I needed to solve for them. I had shared my story. I could finally heal.

MOON MAGIC

Over time, our relationship came to resemble a deep friendship. Sal and I had grown and needed to address new issues in our lives. It was difficult to realize and then accept, and heartbreaking, but a fantastic thing also happened, one that I never would have expected. We didn't break up as much as we agreed that we had grown apart. We talked and discussed the situation in such a mature fashion, addressing each of the concerns that needed to be addressed so that neither of us left wounded. We weren't overly dramatic and extreme, angry or accusatory. What were we going to accuse the other of doing—growing? Healing?

We had obviously found each other for a reason. Now, having helped each other, it was time to acknowledge that the mission had been accomplished and both of us were better from it. We saw that separate paths were being laid out in front of us and the wisest thing for both of us was to acknowledge this reality and pray that whatever came next would be filled with as much care, support, trust, and love that we gave to each other.

"You didn't just love me," I told him. "You taught me how to allow myself to be loved. You made it safe for me to open my heart."

Then I was working on a movie in Canada. It was June 2016, and Sigal emailed me a reminder to honor the upcoming Strawberry Blue Moon. Ever since my experience in Costa Rica, I'd felt a deep connection to the Universe, to Mother Earth and nature. I loved discovering the magic, the little messages in nature. To me, there was a clear connection to the divinity of this existence. It made sense to honor it.

On the night of the blue moon, I drove to a nearby lake. Canada was full of them. It was around midnight when I pulled into the parking lot. I parked my car and walked down to the wooden dock that jutted out from the water house. I'd brought two pieces of paper on which I had written down everything that I didn't want in my life anymore. I knelt on the dock, pulled out some matches, and looked up at the moon in all her glory. With enough light to see the two pieces of paper, I read every line out loud. When I finished, I proceeded to light the pages. As they caught on fire and started to burn, I held them over the lake until they fell away and disappeared into the water.

When they were gone, something in the water caught my eye. It was dark, but with the park lights shining and the glow on the water, I was able to see this creature swimming over to me. Whatever it was, it wasn't in a hurry. It swam leisurely, getting close and taking a good, clear look at me before casually swimming off again. I realized it was a beaver. *Weird,* I thought. Back in my car, I immediately looked up the meaning of this animal totem. It said, "Beaver spirit offers new horizons and hope, particularly with regard to your family and home."

Thank you, little one, I said.

Thank you, Sal.

Thank you, Universe.

Thank you.

HOPE

One day I was on set and walking down a narrow hallway when something caused me to look to my right. In front of me was a young man, and what I noticed most were his eyelashes. They were so unbelievably long! Without considering whether it was appropriate, I stopped and said, "Oh my god, your eyelashes!"

He worked in the art/property department and had been around every day, but until that moment I hadn't noticed him. Then I couldn't stop. My soul had seen him.

"Hi, I'm Mena," I said.

"Mike," he said in return. "Mike Hope."

"Your last name is Hope?" I asked.

"Yeah."

"That's beautiful," I said. "I love it."

The weekend was coming up, and I made plans with my costar to drive down to Toronto and stay with her and her husband. Both of us had to tape auditions and we decided to read and record with each other. It was also going to be nice to get out of the small town where we were filming and spend some time playing in the big city.

On our last night of shooting before the weekend, we worked into the early morning hours. As we wrapped, some of the crew, including Mike, talked about having a beer. I'd kept my eye on him since we had formally met. Interested in being wherever he was, I invited everyone to have that beer in the massive luxury trailer the production had given me. The fun went on until the transportation captain told us that he had to wrap for the weekend and kicked us out. Though it was so late it was actually very early, some of us decided to take the party elsewhere. I ended up driving with Mike and our assistant director down to one of the nearby lakes. The sun was about to come up. We smoked some pot and walked out into the lake to cool our feet off. The water was still, just like our surroundings. It felt peaceful, and I was at ease. I loved my company, and I felt grateful to be where I was, and lucky to feel connected and guided.

We waded in the water for a while and then decided that we'd just call it what it was and stay up. We went to the local coffee shop, ordered breakfast, and sat outside. I was feeling so much attraction toward Mike and a mutual vibe coming back to me that I didn't want the night or the day or whatever it was to end. It was too good to let go.

That's when I mentioned I had to go to Toronto later in the morning. Coincidentally, the assistant director lived there. He had an apartment in the city. Sensing an opportunity, I proposed that we all go together. Someone exclaimed, "Road trip!" and a few hours later we had regrouped, packed, and piled into my car.

Not too far outside of town, we stopped at a beautiful provincial park they recommended we see. There, we set out for a little hike and came upon a magnificent bridge. A bluish-teal color, it stretched across this massive gorge with a sparkling river below. The breeze felt luxurious as I walked across the bridge. The energy in the air, rife with electricity, made my skin tingle. I had a zest for life that was new to me.

Once in Toronto, I stayed with my costar and Mike stayed with our assistant director in his apartment. That night we got together for dinner and drinks. Mike showed me photos he had taken of me standing in the lake water as night gave way to dawn. He captured the air flowing through my hair as we crossed the bridge together and caught me standing within a ray of light between the path and the trees. I had no idea he had taken those photos of me. I was struck by the way I looked. It was a look that reminded me of pictures from my early childhood. I was happy.

I got to know Mike that night and realized the feelings I had in this short time were going to turn into something serious. I had already spoken with Sal before that weekend, but when I got back to LA a couple weeks later, we got together and I told him more about Mike. I cared for Sal so much, and as heartbreaking as it was to look into his eyes and tell him that I thought I was falling in love with another man, I needed to be open and honest with him. He needed to hear it from me.

Then I was ready to explore the connection I had with Mike. I had a tiny bit of time off after we met, but then work picked up and I filmed in Los Angeles and New York City for a long stretch. There was one week when I flew cross-country three times. Toward the end of that blitz, my body broke down and I got sick. After one red-eye to New York, I got off the plane and was taken straight to a local clinic for a steroid shot to get me through the day's work.

After both projects ended, I treated myself to some time off in Ottawa, where Mike was working on a film. Up to this point, we had mostly spent time talking to each other on the phone, but that changed. We had a great home to stay in and went on long walks around Canada's capital city. Ottawa was filled with culture, fresh air, and lovely architecture that made it a splendid backdrop for where the two of us did more than fall in love. We confirmed the long-brewing understanding that what we had was rare, and that we wanted to build on it.

One night, in a beautiful park in the middle of the city, we talked about getting married. Both of us knew that was a wild and crazy idea, but at the same time, it made total sense. Given my track record, I knew it was wise to keep that under wraps for a while and just be together before telling anyone about the commitment we made to each other. But that didn't mean we had to hold back anything from each other. One day Mike and I walked to an awesome overlook, and he got down on his knee and handed me a padlock that he had engraved with the words *Will you marry me?* Of course I accepted, and we clicked it onto the perimeter fence, took the keys, and left our symbol of love there for all to see. *M & M.*

Although we had been together only about three months, I knew it was right. I wasn't against marrying again but I'd truly never thought I would. Having a loving husband and a family was a dream from long ago that I was only just returning to with a sense of possibility and anticipation; I was open to it. And I was sure it was not coincidental that the man who was making me feel this way came with the name Hope.

After Mike's job wrapped, he came to LA for the first time. I took him everywhere, from the beach to boho coffee shops, immersing him into all the things I loved best about the sprawling city. During his next visit, we drove up from Los Angeles to San Francisco and spent a perfect summer weekend at a coastal hideaway I knew from having stayed there as a teenager with my parents and brother. It still oozed the charm I remembered. Before leaving, we decided that it was the perfect place for a wedding.

In August, a day after what would have been my father's birthday, Mike and I exchanged vows in a romantic spot overlooking the Pacific Ocean. Family and friends witnessed our lives change and souls open. I wore a casual dress with a hippie style that I had gotten myself and a crown of flowers I'd found in a local flower shop the day before. Everything felt right, and it truly was the fairy-tale wedding I always wanted.

So began my new life with Mike. We divided our time between Los Angeles and Toronto, where Mike's career was based. Our marriage flourished in parallel with our frequent flier miles. Wherever we were, we took long walks, watched movies, went to concerts, and savored quiet nights at our favorite cafés, where we lingered over drinks and conversation.

I was happiest being with him. His gentle, supportive, loving nature enabled me to continue to feel like I was just beginning to live. Those photographs he took of me the day we stopped at the park when we first met gave me the impression of a butterfly emerging from its cocoon. I continued to get healthy. I exercised, meditated, ate low on the food chain as we both became vegan, and tried to ensure my footprint in the world was gentle and loving.

I reached out to groups where I could talk with teen runaways and survivors of abuse and trauma, people like me who wanted to fight back instead of fighting themselves. Giving back enabled me to see myself better, and what I saw was revelatory. I came to the conclusion that no one had inflicted more damage on me than I did, and that realization was crushing. I had given up on myself. I had believed I wasn't worthy, didn't matter, and thusly wrote myself off. *Do whatever you want with me.*

But no more.

What I wanted was a return to me.

I Am Her

I wish I had just one word to tell you how it feels. I don't and I never will.
So, what is this attempt, then?
I need to heal. I want to heal.
How can I? Have you heard or seen how?
I want her to love me. She always seems too fast for me.

RECLAIMING MY POWER

Starting with my body. In November 2019, I told Michael that I wanted to have my breast implants removed. One of my costars had gone public with the problems she was having with her implants prior to getting them taken out. She had battled infections and then read that the type of implants she had could lead to cancer.

On top of everything else, I was concerned. Michael wrapped his arms around me and was instantly supportive.

"I don't know if I'll ever get back to my real self," I said.

"You are your real self," he said. "And you're constantly doing the work to be your better, healthier self. If this is what you want, I'm with you."

I felt so dumb. I didn't even know the type of implant I had. *In my body!* Ten years had passed since the operation, an amount of time that most people claimed was the cut-off for either replacing the implants or removing them. Over the years, I'd had some issues with my left breast. Scar tissue had grown around the implant, restricting the normal range of motion. I also had problems with my menstrual cycle, weight issues, weird pains—all signs indicating my body was too sensitive to handle the implants, but none of which I'd connected to them at the time.

I met with my doctor who'd done the implants, and who brought a copy of my medical records into the examining room. She put me at ease right away by letting me know the type of implants I had were not the same as those in the cancer study. As we talked and I expressed the fear and shame I felt for not knowing more about what she had put in my body, as well as some other details that gave her more context about my life at the time of the operation, my doctor said, "I wish I had tried to talk you out of it. At least given you more affirmation that you were—and are—wonderful."

"I think that's my responsibility," I said. "It's my responsibility to learn my lessons. The way I look at it, I had the best doctor helping me achieve what I was looking for then, and now I have the best doctor helping me achieve what I want now."

We talked more about the first operation before I asked what I would look like if I were to take them out.

"You'll look like you," she said. "It's not that much time or money."

Afterward, I had a long talk with Michael, who was aware of my vacillating insecurities about my body. He said the decision was mine, but he made it clear that I needed to do it for myself. My appearance didn't matter to him, he said. He loved me, not an image of me or a version of me that I wanted to be.

"When I say, 'I love you,' I mean *you*," he said.

I had the surgery on December 26, 2019. The procedure didn't take long, and everything went according to plan. As they wheeled me out of the operating room, I turned my head to the side and saw the two implants in a dish next to my head. *Bye-bye*, I thought. I was so damn proud they were out. I was myself again. Although the next battle would be hoping it would look okay. And if it didn't? The test came a few months later when a woman left a snarky comment on my Instagram page.

For much of my life, her comment would have destroyed me. And it did make me upset—upset that I hadn't ever been strong enough to love myself as I was. Now, I wanted to feel as perfectly imperfect, awkward, and unique as I came into the world. I wanted to rediscover myself and reclaim my power. I wanted to continue to heal and learn to love myself, so I could love my husband the way he deserved and, eventually, hopefully, start a family that we would raise and nurture in a way that would allow them to live their lives with confidence, an open heart, hope, kindness, and love . . .

Love . . .

Love . . .

TRUTH

Over the years I have given hundreds of interviews and never mentioned anything about the dark part of my life.

The stories in this book mark the first time I have shared the details of these years of sexual and emotional abuse and the effects that followed me well into adulthood. I tried to write with the courage, fearlessness, and honesty that kept me alive. I hope it can have the same effect on those who need to find a story like mine to give them hope—hope that they can survive abuse and trauma and hope from realizing they are not alone.

Coming upon the suicide note I wrote began the process for me. "Take care," it said toward the end. "I'll see you again someday. Make the most of what you have and remember you're never alone." It took me twenty years to find that letter, but that was the day I saw myself again, as I had once written, and began this process of healing. I always thought I was healing, but only when I read that note did I begin to face every moment that came before and stop running away from the past and begin to truly heal.

It was time to tell my story. I was inspired by the courageous women who went public with their stories as part of the #MeToo movement, and I was equally if not more inspired by those who came forward with their stories of abuse for reasons other than #MeToo but were not believed. Above all else, I was inspired and indeed compelled to share my story by all the people who were like me, gripped by fear and denial and suffering in silence. Yet, there was still a lot of work I needed to do in order to get out of my own way and be vulnerable enough to write.

One day I went into my office with a cup of coffee and a handful of courage, opened my computer, and laid my fingers on the keyboard. I said a silent prayer and gave myself permission to remember, to speak, to exercise my voice. I didn't know if anything would come out, if I could put words on the page. To my surprise, the words poured out of me. The feeling grew into something awesome, difficult, painful, purposeful, and freeing.

Between the ages of twelve and twenty, I was the victim of repeated sexual abuse. It continued for years, defining my future relationships. Like many such victims of sexual abuse, I conflated feelings of shame and anger with affection. As I grew up, I gravitated toward men who took advantage of my vulnerability and confusion. A photographer. A manager. A lighting engineer. I assumed each unhappy stop was my fault. I got what I deserved. I didn't know life could be different. I felt powerless to change.

I took drugs to numb myself from the pain. Alcohol. Pot. Coke. Crystal meth. Acid. Ecstasy. Mushrooms. Mescaline. It was my way of detaching from the hell of my existence—and surviving. As my career took off, this life of mine was my secret—my secret world of shame, embarrassment, and guilt. As an actress, it was easy for me to be the person other people thought or wanted me to be. I slipped into whatever role was required and safe, including two marriages that served as ill-conceived escapes. In many ways, art saved my life.

In the meantime, my real self was a shadow in hiding, someone I knew was there, someone with value and potential but also a fragile, broken soul in need of help. I couldn't reach her. It was crippling—until finally, after escaping into two bad marriages, I met loving individuals who helped me see and understand it didn't have to be that way.

I have come to believe that the most important thing we can do with one another is share our experiences and try to help and teach and inspire one another. Our culture is geared around tearing others down. I believe we should lead with kindness. The only path to our greatest peace is through an open heart.

I am grateful that I was able to meet up again with my sixteen-year-old self and help her understand that the terrible pain she suffered was her greatest gift. She gave me my voice, and now I am giving her a voice—the voice that those of us caught up in this suffering are brainwashed to believe we don't have. I want this book to provide companionship to those who are isolated and alone. I hope it can be a light showing there is a way out. I never want anyone to look at me, or anyone else who has gone through similar experiences, and ask, *How could you let that happen to you—and not just once but repeatedly?* It's not our fault.

I spent a lifetime hiding from the truth.

Then I discovered that truth was my power.

Truth is our power.

ACKNOWLEDGMENTS

First and foremost, all my love to the Universe for continuing to guide me. For always carrying me through this wild journey of life by bringing in those shining lights that I needed at just the right time, some of which are listed here.

To everyone who helped make this book possible: my literary agent, Dan Strone at Trident Media Group, and to my editor, Ben Schafer, and everyone at Hachette Books. Thank you for giving me the opportunity to share my story.

To Chuck James, for seeing something in me that I never saw in myself and working tirelessly to build it while supporting me so incredibly in my personal life.

To Oren Segal, my extraordinary manager and brother-from-another. Without you, I never would have met Todd Gold, who urged me to take on this project—one of the biggest of my life. Thank you for always having my best interest in mind and encouraging me to write my truth.

To my friends—my "family," who carried me through every dark night, and who stood by and supported me unconditionally: Jennie, Nicole, Stephanie, Gabby, Tracy, Sigal, and Suzanne. And those not mentioned in these chapters, who helped me believe that the work on this book would be meaningful: Jana "Shirls," Elana, Elisa, Sara, Bobby, Nola, Jen, Allyson, Phyllis, and Brevi. Thank you.

To my blood—my mother and father, for giving me life, and my brothers who shared childhood with me, guiding and supporting me as best they could. Thank you for showing love and putting in the effort to help me succeed.

And lastly but most importantly, to my husband, Michael—my Hope, the one who brought new life into my existence. You showed me what could be possible for me in finally finding happiness. And you helped bring our beautiful angel, Christopher, into our lives. I believe this journey has only ever been to find you, my son. And should you read this book one day, know that I always felt you by my side guiding me toward the light.